McFarland
Classics

Bad at the Bijou

William R. Horner

McFarland & Company, Inc., Publishers
Jefferson, North Carolina, and London

Frontispiece: Lee Van Cleef pensive with pipe, *The Big Gundown*, 1968.

Library of Congress Cataloguing-in-Publication Data

Horner, William R., 1949–
    Bad at the Bijou.
    Filmography: p.
    Includes index.
    ISBN 0-7864-0938-X (softcover : 60# alkaline paper) ∞
    1. Villains in motion pictures. I. Title.
PN1995.9.V47H67   2000   791.43'09'09353   82-17222

British Library cataloguing data are available

McFarland & Company, Inc., Publishers
   Box 611, Jefferson, North Carolina 28640
     www.mcfarlandpub.com

*To my wife Nancy,
who always wears the white hat*

Table of Contents

I

Who Is That Man
Behind the Frosty Grunts?

Picture an archaeological dig in the year 4000. Professor X.Y. Zee, esteemed anthropologist, is studying artifacts from our era with the same care we would treat newfound relics of Imperial Rome. He has happened across a motion picture film in mint condition. Assuming no catastrophe will have intervened that caused man to regress technologically, Zee will be able to run the long, flexible strip through some kind of device to analyze his find.

The English language did not exist in A.D. 1, and since its present version will probably be gibberish in A.D. 4000, our future antiquarian will be working in translation. After the credits have flashed before him, he jots them down, consults a few musty references, and determines that before him is a print of *Rooster Cogburn*, a John Wayne opus from 1976. The tale it spins for Zee is of the title character, and how he runs afoul of preacherwoman Eula Goodnight. Hawk's gang stormed through the church mission run by her brother, scattered their timid Indian flock and, right before Eula's eyes, Hawk shot down Reverend Goodnight like a dog.

Deputy U.S. Marshal Cogburn rides into the wasted mission with better things to do, but resigns himself to escort Eula and her young Indian friend Wolf to safety. Halfway through the film this doughty trio manage to recapture a stolen wagonload of dynamite, ammunition, and a Gatling gun from one of Hawk's several dull-witted henchmen. Their story becomes a race between Rooster, who tries to reach an army fort with his charges and the deadly freight, and Hawk, who tries to overtake them.

Circumstances force Rooster, Eula and Wolf to load their cargo on a raft and head for the fort by a treacherous water route. Hawk's underlings harry them with potshots from shore. Taking care to miss the explosives, they try to knick the one-eyed lawman's tall silhouette. Downstream, the heavily weighted raft bobs in the wild river's froth and nearly smashes itself against steep canyon walls.

Eula and Rooster propitiate in their own ways. She prays, and he swears to give up whiskey. Something works. They survive the ordeal, if just barely. In calm waters they take a long breath and find all cargo intact; and yet, no miracle has arisen to spare them from Hawk's clutches, which they know is their fate just around the bend at a fording spot.

Sweet inspiration! Eula and Wolf dump crates of dynamite overboard, while Rooster slows the raft's progress and allows the cases to gain distance in the current. As expected, the outlaws wait for them on horseback in a line across the shallows. Rooster ducks out of sight.

Noting all the flotsam, Hawk taunts Eula about their difficult passage. And where's Cogburn? he inquires. He's hurt, Eula tells him, and needs a doctor. Hawk promises to help, but leers to his fellows, meaning: No quarter!

Crafty Eula exchanges shouts with the bandits downstream, but under her breath she counsels Rooster as the crates float nearer, nearer the outlaws. Once the dynamite lazes in the water close about the horses, she summons him up.

Rooster sights down the barrel of his Winchester and fires into the crates. Faster than the eye can follow, the explosives ignite and catch up the gang in a giant ball of fire and vapor. It's as if the Duke had dropped a tactical nuke on their heads. When the smoke clears, there is nothing left of Hawk or his minions.

In the year 4000, how will all this be read? Assuming again that despite man's best efforts, information becomes lost through natural disasters and other unthinkable calamities, our Professor Zee may lack some of history's connective tissue. Details of 19th century life on the American frontier may have sunk to the bottom of time's murky duck pond, and he might have no idea what to make of Rooster or Eula or Hawk. Did this video recording claim to represent real historical figures? Or were they larger-than-life fantasies? If Zee were compiling his own version of *The Golden Bough*, he might suspect the film of bearing certain earmarks of mythology—a river passage, a cyclops, a priestess, an acolyte, fire-spitting scepters, a boxed-up power almost magical in its destructiveness. At least there is one assessment of *Rooster Cogburn* that would be so familiar to Zee that he could have presupposed it: For the benefit of an audience, a contest was contrived between a force or condition of "good" against one of "evil."

Even if whole passages of dialogue defied translation or the soundtrack would not adapt itself at all to any given apparatus and *Cogburn* ran as a silent film, even Zee's contemporaries ultimately would have to sympathize with its protagonists, despise Hawk for his rapacity and treachery, and welcome Hawk's ghastly demise. Unless the bulk of mankind changes immediately in some fundamental way, this moralizing through a staging of mock violence will continue frequently enough for Professor Zee to be aware of it up to his own day; and depending on the wealth of his resources, he will certainly recognize that this sort of dramatic fare preceded 1976, too far back into man's prehistory for the discovery of one more example in *Rooster Cogburn* to shock him.

So much for perspective. By jumping twenty centuries ahead, taking the long view only adds a minute or two on our time card as a species; but at least it serves to illustrate a constancy in man for which plentiful examples can be cited, examples that are not lost from our own museums, archives and libraries through decay or mishap. Of practically any culture known to us in any given historical period or geographic setting, one could read how that culture has created for itself a system of values where a consensus has formed on the meaning of "good" and "evil." Whenever man goes to curry favor from the supernatural, to perform an official function within his community, or simply to be entertained; that moral consensus colors the event. He is reassured by watching his fundamental values — those that are life-sustaining, orderly, noble, preferred — battle with and prevail over those that are frightening and repugnant. He is comforted to see positive champions conquer or expel negative forces, or at times turn physical defeat into "moral victory." This is something we should keep in mind before we cluck, and shake our heads over a film or television show in which persuasion is less than friendly, characters are unsavory, or guns go off and bodies drop. Fitted into the whole dramatic spectrum, they are not unusual.

Oddly enough, the means of Hawk's disposal in the climax of *Rooster Cogburn* has a "legitimate" parallel that takes place yearly in New Delhi. In the Hindu festival called the Navaratri, a half-dozen gigantic demon effigies are put to the torch, representing the victory of Rama, seventh incarnation of the god Vishnu, over the ten-headed, twenty-armed demon king Ravana. Although manlike figures of wood, canvas and papier-mache substitute for live actors and their combustion is not as instantaneous as dynamite's, the fate of Ravana's demons matches the enormous pillar of smoke engulfing Hawk's gang, and multiplies it by six. On reflecting, as the Hindus believe, that the effigies suffer vicariously for real demon counterparts, we sense what a horrible manner of execution it is; and yet, two independent groups of people for their own dissimilar reasons have made a display of it, and hordes of festival celebrants and ticket buyers are eager to observe.

Probing deeper into this matter of spectacles where bitter adversaries meet and one side falls, we would find among the Arundas of Australia a primitive ritual once performed to introduce pubescent boys to facts of their tribal history. Their ancestor was the kangaroo, they would be told. They were descended from kangaroo-men whose enemies were dingo-men. With this introduction, two figures appeared. They were tribesmen with small *waninga*'s — bones carved with sacred images — affixed to their hair, and except for the *waninga*'s and their human forms, nothing else distinguished them as men. Their movements and sounds were masterpieces of animal mimicry. They craned their necks in a wary search for predators. Their lips clenched sticks, and their hair was sprinkled with wood shavings, all stained red to symbolize wounds already suffered in battles with the dingo. Eventually they encountered a dingo-man lying asleep on his side. He, too, would act more animal than human, springing up on all fours, yelping, and lunging with bared teeth. In the end, the kangaroos seized their foe between themselves and shook him. The dingo-man howled in moribund agony as they dashed his head against the ground until he was silent and limp.

The aftermath of combat played an important role in a rite of passage among the Fiji islanders. During a period of basic military training, adolescent boys were marshalled into the heavily wooded uplands and taught to make hardwood spears and bamboo knives. A *vere*, a skilled elder warrior, would conduct their instruction, and lead them one night into a clearing where at the far end there stood a pandanus mat hut with a peaked roof of thatched savanna grass. By his breast ornaments of sea shell and cachalot ivory the boys recognized their chief glaring at them with what appeared to be a rage just barely contained. Several small campfires lit their approach to the hut, where two rows of warriors — the boys' uncles and fathers — faced one another, dressed for battle and wearing necklaces of human teeth representative of combat kills. The men flanked a barrier that from a distance resembled fallen logs, vaguely humanoid in shape. The *vere* lined the boys up to confront it.

Six men of their village lay dead before them. The boys had hunted wild boar, butchered dogs for meat, and treated ambulatory wounded come back from skirmishes, but they never saw the mortally injured and dead who were left on the field of battle, never to bring home the shame of their personal military defeat. The dead mouths gaped, the dead eyes stared or showed gruesomely white. Dirt mixed with gore caked the dead men's bodies, and entrails decorated their mutilated chests. The *vere* led each boy, singly forcing him to pick his way slowly through the twisted limbs over the blood-sodden earth while pieces of viscera squiggled under his bare feet. Each boy had ample time to absorb the grisly sight. Once they had all traversed the carnage, they trembled under the wilting gaze of their chief. Suddenly he screamed, and unworldly yells chimed in behind them. The unnerved boys dropped their spears as the "cadavers" staggered around them howling, singing, and finally making a dash for a stream to wash off the blood and guts of chickens and swine.

Another simulated death-and-revival crops up among American Indians of the Northwestern Plateau. Candidates for the bear totem stepped forward in a longhouse full of chanting lodge members. In the torrid atmosphere made nearly suffocating from a cloud of smoldering herbs, the candidate would doff his bark poncho and, by all appearances, the medicine man gouged him savagely with a ritual spear. The initiate crumpled to the packed earth floor gurgling real blood as if his heart had actually been pierced, but gradually rose to his feet as drums restored a heartbeat in his body and his lodge brothers sang him back to life. At ceremony's end, the bear totem's new member spat out a crushed sac of

4

deer's blood, and the medicine man tweezed a retractable spear point from the haft of his ceremonial lance.

As the arts and rituals of our "civilized" kinsmen would imply, the knack for settling conflicts peaceably or for symbolizing transitions through genteel imagery are notions no more at home with us than they were among "savages." During the Anthesteria, a Dionysian festival observed at the end of February by the ancient Greeks, Athenians assumed that souls of the dead infested their city. Ghosts crowded the streets and courtyards. Progenitors returned to mingle with their descendants. Families set a place at the table for recently departed members. Unfortunately, not only good spirits, but evil ones had reappeared and would attempt possession of living bodies by darting in through open mouths. As the festival amounted to little more than a three-day binge, zealous obeisance to the wine god provided celebrants ample protection by raising against the malevolent ghosts a constant barricade of tilted goblets.

On the final day, guardians of Dionysian ritual assembled large bands of men and women. To restore normalcy in Athens, those entities who could never again be made to bleed or die, both friendly and wicked, had to be banished and driven back to the grave. Choric dancers draped themselves from head to foot in white diaphanous robes. Bleary-eyed citizens looked down from rooftops at the clatter in the streets winding out of Athens to outlying cemeteries as the dancers retreated from a howling mob that beat swords against bucklers, twirled staves, and swept the pavement with besoms. The sweepers swung their twig brooms straight outward and up, as if to snap wisps of former life from the air. "Be off!" the mob shouted. "Be off, ye ghosts! The Anthesteria is over." Soberly, gracefully the wraith-like dancers mimed a pain and reluctance felt by those real, unseen specters who at the very head of the procession fled from the clamor of the living.

Not even the medieval "morality play" will shield us from rough-house and ranch, despite its Sunday school clean-sounding label. Church literature and sermons of that era burgeoned with graphic accounts of the war between forces of Good and Evil for the prizes of Man's Soul, and moralities reflected this martial analogy in their plots. *The Psychomachia*, a stirring epic by the 4th century Roman poet Prudentius, became a model for numerous tracts, sermons and plays as it allegorized in female characters the Seven Deadly Sins and their seven goodly, unassuming, heavenly opposites. In the course of their bloody encounter, Faith impaled Heathenry, Chastity skewered the neck of Lust with a sword, Patience drove Wrath to suicide by disembowelment, Humility slit the throat of Pride, Sobriety hacked Luxury to pieces, Good Works throttled and knifed Greed, and Concord rammed a javelin down the gullet of Heresy.

One derivative of *The Psychomachia* is *The Castle of Perseverance*, the earliest morality play whose complete text has survived. Here again the Virtues are characterized by seven righteous women. They defend

Man in the fortress of Perseverance which comes under siege from the Bad Angel, the World, Flesh, the Devil, and the Seven Vices. Touring players presented the attack as authentically as possible, and were we to visit a production of *Perseverance*, say in 1416, we would see the figurative mayhem get a hearty reception. It was not a tame era, and *Perseverance* did not play to a squeamish audience. Hardly an adult or child existed who had never seen a whipping post, gibbet or headsman's block put to use; and as adversaries traded blows across the castle battlements with real swords, their steel rang a familiar tune.

This generation of Englishmen had known of, or fought in the Welsh and Hotspur uprisings, or the Battle of Agincourt of the year before. Everyone from the lowest commoner to lords and ladies convulsed with laughter at the raucous combat before them, and cheered as Vices spilled heavily to the stage from their scaling ladders. Through sleight-of-hand while writhing on the boards, the actors anointed themselves with bloody pigments and smeared "bruises" on their faces. While the play occurred with consent from the church and opened with blessings from a priest, much of its coarse banter would not align with our own standards of wholesomeness. Pride, for instance, eyed the virtuous ladies atop the castle walls and sniggered:

> "To Goliath I make a vow
>   For to strike each yonder trollop.
> On her arse, torn and rough,
>   I shall both clatter and wallop."

Gluttony promised:

> "Those bitches shall go pale and blubber;
> I shall make such a choke,
> Both with smolder and with smoke,
>   They shall shit from fear."

Lechery flaunted herself before her opposite and huffed:

> "Lo, Chastity, thou foul tart!
>   This very day here thou shalt die.
> I make a flame in man's arse
>   That springs up as any fire.
> These cursed coils I bear about
>   Mankind in grief to tie.
> Men and women hath, no doubt,
>   With pissing parts for to play."

Finally when the tide of battle turned against them, the Vices retreated and the Bad Angel was forced to scream at his infernal troops:

> "Yea, the Devil speed you, every bit!
> For sorrow I moan on the ground.
> I carp, I cry, I crouch, I shit,
> I fret, I fart, I fizzle foul,
> I look like an owl."

For two centuries, beginning with the reign of Richard II and lasting halfway into that of Elizabeth I, morality plays out-drew all other forms of theater in Britain and across the Continent. Dogmatic trimmings notwithstanding, their rousing tiffs between Good and Bad kept them alive long enough to plant seeds of even greater moral conflicts in the mind of a young William Shakespeare. Ironically *The Castle of Perseverance* today could never be viewed on television in its original form, or at the movies without a restricted rating.

Look not to the East. The highly regarded Kabuki theater of Japan has a tradition of the shocking and bizarre. Originated as a dramatic form in 1586, Kabuki theaters could be found in the pleasure quarters of major cities alongside gambling dens and geisha houses, and sex and violence characterized the bulk of their offerings. Playwrights merely converted the realities of contemporary urban living — murders, amorous suicide pacts, vendettas, oppressive administrators and cruel warriors — into erotic melodramas and exciting tales of strife. Audiences could enjoy the dramatization of some familiar current event, although the prominent family involved or the scandalized government official was thinly disguised with fictional names, and the action would be relegated to a distant time and place.

The Daimyo, a play written and performed in the late 18th century, is an exemplary piece from Kabuki. Jiro Danyemon, the daimyo (ruling provincial prince), has been absent from the cottage where his 16-year-old concubine had attempted to seduce a young itinerant Shinto monk. Once at home, Jiro deduces from Namiko's incomplete tidying that she had been entertaining a young man. In a rage he chases her off-stage, neatly slicing his sword through the door she draws between them.

In the climactic scene, the monk Yasui returns to the cottage. A lantern is burning that Namiko told him she would light if the daimyo were away. He enters the cottage. All signs of violence have been repaired. He sees Namiko kneeling over a low table. He speaks. She does not reply. Thinking she may be drowsy, he gives her arm a nudge. Her head separates from her shoulders, rolls off the table, and across the room. Horrified, he rushes to the severed head and carries it into the light, hoping he will not see the face of his almost-lover. A door to the rear glides open. Jiro grins ominously. In the words of the stage directions out of *The Daimyo*'s text, "The moon, which had been slowly setting, disappears; and nothing remains but darkness, leaving the audience to awake gradually, as from a painful dream."

We could find swordplay in a more incongruous setting, such as the staid parlor of a home in Victorian England. In the Cornish town of Camborne, certain villagers strolled throughout their city garishly painted and quaintly garbed as mummers to perform the village Christmas play wherever there was room to hold their troupe and a small audience. These mummers were no lighthearted gang of feathered and spangled banjo players, thrumming "Oh, Dem Golden Slippers" as they went. As we might expect at Yuletide, their master of ceremonies was a rotund gentleman with a billowing set of fake white whiskers, a fur-trimmed coat, and a lively timbre in his voice; but his was not the image of jolly, coddly, commercialized philanthropy. His face was painted a startling crimson with dusky eyes and stern, upsweeping brows. This was the Father Christmas of bad children's nightmares, the bringer of switches and ashes.

The Camborne mummers retold a meeting between George, Patron Saint of England, and the Turkish Knight. The Infidel stormed into the playing area brandishing a wooden scimitar and crowing:

> "I came from the Turkish land to fight:
> First I fought in England,
> And then I fought in Spain,
> And now I am come back to England
> To fight St. George again.
> If I could meet St. George here,
> I would put my spear in through his ear,
> I would beat him and bale him
> And cut him in slices
> And take a small pot
> And make a pair of garters."

To this challenge St. George responded:

> "Here comes I St. George
> A man of courage bold:
> If thy blood is hot
> I will soon make it cold,
> As cold as any clay;
> I will take thy blood and life away."

They fought, cracking the flats of their swords together while their fellow mummers scampered for safety. The Turk sustained a fatal gash, was revived briefly by a gnomish doctor — portrayed by a 12-year-old boy who claimed, "I can cure the itch, the specks, the spots and the gout; if there's nine devils in, I can kick ten out" — but fell again under St. George's blows. The Devil came in, hoisted the corpse up onto his back head downward, and the dead Turk's accusative eyes raked over the audience as he was carried out. His macabre stare mesmerized them so, it would take a moment for them to realize the drama was over.

What is all this if not the same old rite, the same dance, the same chant, the same mummery? It is the "good guys" versus the "bad guys," meeting the definitions of those terms, of course, relative to each individual locale. The little dramas in this sampler of mock violence are hardly interchangeable among the separate cultures. For example, it is difficult for us not to sympathize with *The Daimyo*'s young lovers Yasui and Namiko. Yasui is much more suited to the girl than Jiro Danyemon, who is a much older man, officially married to another woman, and capriciously cruel. Nor do we Americans, unlike the Arundas, encourage one another to think of ourselves as bald eagle-men, bearing a shoulder-chip in the presence of other nationalities. Still, what might offend our sensibilities in these scenarios performed an important function within their own communities. *The Daimyo* affirmed the convictions of a society where the rights of the military ruling class were held unassailable. The sight of ancestral struggle filled Arunda boys with a sense of self-worth, and increased their will to survive and perpetuate their own kind in a harsh environment. The Arunda and Fijian initiations were thought indispensable for converting adolescents into competent food gatherers and protectors. The morality play propagated tenets of the church to a largely illiterate flock of parishioners.

Perhaps even more importantly, operating more on a psychological level than social, each play or rite disposes of some negative condition or concept; in effect, exorcises it from the community. For the Hindus at the Navaratri, it was demons. For the Arundas, dingo-men. The blood-spattered "corpses" of Fiji symbolized military ineptitude, the wrong path, the way not to go if a boy wished to fulfill his manly obligations. The Indian bear totem ceremony was almost Christian in theme with its killing of the "Old Man" and a rise from death of a "New Man," freshly certified and ready to follow higher precepts. The Athenians purged their city of the dread shadow of Death. Yasui had to pay for straying—even slightly—from his priestly vows, and to suffer with Namiko for their effrontery to Jiro Danyemon, infinitely their social superior. *Perseverance* urged its viewers to spurn traffic with the Seven Deadly Sins. The Camborne mummers' play, while presented at Christmas time, had little to do with the Holy Infant so tender and mild. Its real roots lay buried in pre-Christian vegetation rites. In the original version of pagan Britain, "Father Christmas" was Father Time. His "son," the Turk, was the Old Year whom the New Year must kill at winter solstice to make way for seasonal changes and the continued cycle of life.

This brings us down to the nub. The essence of drama is conflict. No story can hold the attention of its gathered audience without showing a problem to override. If a child finds a large beetle on the sidewalk, he may be satisfied to watch the insect's natural habits for a few minutes, but it won't be long before he is laying a twig in its path to see how the beetle will react. Will he circumnavigate, or clamber over the top?

As drama involves our sympathy, we identify with the protagonist, the hero. We root for him, feel for him, fear for him, pull for him in whatever predicament the story has cast him. Conflict usually originates from a human agent. Consequently, unless the story pits its characters against the impersonal forces of nature, there is always a heavy. It doesn't matter if we are watching a drawing room comedy on stage or a thriller movie, there is always some character — an imbecilic fop, a sniper amuck in the big city — who draws our disfavor.

American movies have fed our insatiable appetite for heroes. It may be a chicken-or-egg question whether Hollywood has created an artificial demand that feeds on itself, or whether movies copy from life a genuine heroism in real frontiersmen, soldiers, statesmen, artists, sports figures, or girls and boys next door; but for years Hollywood has cranked out a steady supply of heroes in its television and film productions. Inevitably an actor who plays the protagonist is deemed the "star" of the piece. If he does this often enough, he becomes a star, period, and the media will not confine their scrutiny to his work, but pursue him off camera and into his private life. A star's take-home salary for a single year will rival the lifetime earnings of his average fan. His name dominates posters and marquees, gets top billing in film credits, and sometimes even takes precedence over the title of his dramatic vehicle. So much of our attention focuses on film and television stars and their work, these facts are common knowledge. About heroes we know plenty.

More to the sidelines of Hollywood, away from the limelight of public adulation, stand a host of co-stars and supporting actors. When a film or teleplay dictates, they stand in opposition to the star, providing stark contrast between their own character and that of the protagonist's; and just as legendary heroes achieved fame not by the mere swatting of flies, but by slaying giants, the better supporting actors have lent a touch of gianthood to their villainy. Without them, lead characters would not appear so endangered and heroic and a film would not be half as capable of rivetting an audience to its seat. With the assistance of makeup and wardrobe for twisted physiognomy or the look of filthiness; or through their own physical attributes, such as a powerful physique; or by their inventiveness as actors in the exhibition of psychopathy, bigotry or sadism, they project from their roles a dangerous aura of moral deficiency. Since the late sixties when the film industry created a rating system to screen children from its harshest products, depictions of violence and sexual activities have never been so graphic; and it is unlikely that we have ever seen villains more antisocial, more ugly, more brutal.

It might be noted that outright heroes and villains are not as plentiful as they once were. The B western is dead. Just as a film's protagonist commonly arrives in the form of an "antihero" — sometimes an abrasive, belligerent character, sometimes a lawbreaker, nearly always "alienated" — there also exist varying degrees of villainy. Because of the mature manner with which our entertainments have come to treat character and theme, nowadays we are as likely to encounter a charming knave as an ogre on screen. The villain of a piece may be deemed a "light heavy," or his vices may be submerged to the point that his is only a "character part." A shady secondary character can even be sympathetic, winning our favor through close association with an antiheroic protagonist. Like the antihero he may be an utter scoundrel, or perhaps he is only mildly distasteful. This clouds the issue of exactly what constitutes a "heavy," and a working definition should be established at this point, a definition which encompasses the actors selected for study within these pages. It is a general one, necessitated by the complexities of modern cinema — but the final litmus test for a heavy is this: Regardless of his moral stripe or sympathetic coloration within the context of a story, a heavy's deviations from the social norm exclude him from the mainstream of society. We may string along with him in the theater's darkness, but we cannot completely merge our identity with his. Stepping out in the light of day, we realize we would not swap the security of our homes, families and jobs for his life as a sidewalk down-and-out, saddle tramp, petty criminal, venal public official, invincible tough or the like, temporarily colorful though it may seem to us. Even if he is a sympathetic tag-along behind the lead character, his secondary stature relative to the hero's (or antihero's) would not make an exchange of places worth our while.

However we regard him, whatever name we use to describe his character — "light villain," "lead heavy," "baddie," "sympathetic heavy" — despite standout performances by some of Hollywood's most visible heavies, film critics seldom call them anything at all. Their labors pass with small note, and their names do not rest on the tongue-tips of an admiring throng. Possibly the types of roles they draw — peripheral, unglamorous, sometimes that of an outright pariah — transfer their negativity to the actors, leaving the impression that they are less deserving of consideration than other elements of a picture. Whatever the drawbacks, they continue to roam the movie-television circuit playing a variety of badmen and sinister personalities, often escorting spectators, who squirm and fret over the predicament of the heavy's victims, across the thresholds of pain to death's door; gouging at a survival instinct that has gone nearly dormant in a sheltered, pampered, privileged viewing public. While this has not made them household words, many of their screen creations brand images into the mind, refusing to vacate the memory; and their sparse lines of dialogue or bits of business come back to haunt us like bad dreams.

When little boys used to play cowboys and Indians or cops and robbers, the ones who wound up as Indians or robbers at first would pout and sulk, because by the end of the game they would have to lie in itchy grass and play dead. That was the prevailing morality, and their only hope to prolong participation was through litigation. Terrific arguments would spring up between two boys yelling at the tops of their lungs, "No, *I* shot *you* first." Most of us are the same way. We identify with movie stars and protagonists. If we fancy ourselves in a cinematic situation, we choose an appealing role, not a dastardly one. We long for the attention, the approval, the adulation that are a star's due.

But who are these men so often sporting a gruff voice or a stubbled face, a hair-trigger temper or the sneer of fickle allegiance in the guise of a villain? They are actors, but aside from the efflux of publicity mills, the scandalmongery of tabloids and the prattle of celebrities on variety talk shows, does the public have an accurate picture of what an "actor" is? How did the heavies happen into so many negative roles, some of them playing villains and sinisters to the exclusion of all other type parts? Do *they* sulk or pout when once again they draw the villain's lot? If so, how do they manage to throw themselves into each new part with the same amount of verve as went into the role before? Do they yearn to play straight characters, or for the chance to be romantic leads? What goes into the making of a tempestuous imitation of violence? Where does the personality of a screen villain end, and the actor's begin? Where do they overlap?

For a dozen-odd years from the mid-sixties to the late seventies, movies showed unprecedented extremes of seaminess and brutality. While this period is still a fresh memory, such inquiries are hardly insignificant; for the skills of this unique caste of performers are partly responsible for the impact of such films. Moreover, they are the legal heirs of a banner handed down from the ghosts of Athens, the assailants of Perseverance, the dingo-men, and St. George's Turkish adversary. Their traditions are ancient and formidable. Their place among us is honorable, and the relative obscurity surrounding them—compared with their better known, better paid colleagues—is undeserved.

It is the purpose of *Bad at the Bijou* to lift this veil of obscurity. As it will soon become plain, there is no single answer to the questions listed above. There are scores of sources one could canvass for answers in order to form a fairly accurate picture of the Hollywood character-heavy's peculiar niche in the entertainment field. Of these scores, many are quite good actors; but it would be hard to imagine any finer than the ten men collected herein, and interviewed by phone as they became available between early 1976 and late 1979. It is hoped that their words will cast some light onto filmdom's peripheries where the heavy works and lives.

It is no less intended that these chapters offer the chance for some very special actors to take a long overdue bow.

II

Bad as They Come

"Let me have men about me that are fat,
Sleek-headed men, and such as sleep a-nights.
Yond Cassius has a lean and hungry look.
He thinks too much. Such men are dangerous."
Act One, Scene II, *Julius Caesar*

Jack Elam is not a Shakespearean actor, nor could most of his film or television characters be accused of thinking too much or, at least, too deeply. Still, he has played many dangerous men whose appetites for violence and cruelty were wolfish. The reputation he has built from these countless villains makes him one of the few heavies who truly needs no introduction.

All during the fifties and early sixties, Jack Elam typified the Western badman with his tall, lank frame, his swarthy countenance, Mephistophelean brows, and drilling gaze. This rather fixed image derives from the fact that of his more than 50 movies, three-fourths are Westerns and, up until 1969 with a sympathetic and uproariously funny portrayal in *Support Your Local Sheriff*, a predominance of his characters were the worst of bad apples. He has since been dealt a greater variety of roles, however, most typically as an irascible cuss with a heart of gold (10-karat). Extra poundage and a thick beard have taken rough edges off the slack jaw and wiriness of his cleanshaven days, and he has become a grandfatherly scene stealer, masterfully strumming the coy heartstrings of his audience. But then, this is no new trick for Elam, whose charms—like those of a cobra hypnotizing its victim—have commanded unwavering attention since his earliest shady walk-ons.

Jack Elam joined the film industry not as an actor, but as an accountant. As a young man he ran down jobs in Southern California wherever he could put himself through school. After finishing business studies at Modesto and Santa Monica junior colleges he became an auditor for Samuel Goldwyn studios, and acted as comptroller for several companies, among them Hopalong Cassidy Productions. It was not an ideal occupation for someone who, as a boy, had lost vision in one eye. Poring over ledgers and reports so overtaxed his remaining sighted eye that a doctor gave Elam the choice of abandoning his profession or going totally blind. Elam just happened to be in position to switch from working behind film cameras to performing in front of them; which alternative, at the time, was as much a leap into darkness.

Compared with the route into movies many of his peers had taken, Jack Elam's sudden status as a Thespian was something of a shortcut. Most actors learn their trade through a long apprenticeship in live theater. Steeped in the fundamentals of drama, going all the way back to Greek tragedies with a lingering look at Shakespeare, many actors are heard to utter statements about their vocation as an "art" and about themselves as "artists." They echo Aristotle's idea of drama as a "catharsis" for the audience, incorporating this in their own attempts to live out the emotions of their assumed characters. This preparation holds true, undoubtedly, for most of our finest actors; but its absence from Elam's background hardly seems to have hampered the quality of his work. Besides, in our conversation by telephone, Elam deftly brushed aside such traditional notions as applied to his career. Queried about his acting experience prior to surrendering his green eyeshade—college plays? ... little theater?—he replied flatly, "None. I do not do live theater. I have no interest in doing theater. I've had offers from New York and other legitimate places, but it is not my line. I am strictly a film actor."

"But how do you view your efforts? Do you consider yourself an artist," I asked, "and have you been satisfied with the chances you've had for artistic achievement? Or do you simply see a role as equalling a paycheck?"

"I consider that term 'artist' completely too pretentious," he objected, "and I'm *totally* satisfied with the opportunities I've had for any artistic achievement. I don't live the role-equals-paycheck thing, but I am *not* an *artist*. I am a *man* who is *paid* to do *acting*. It is my *profession*," he declared. "As a result, that gets me to work on time. I take my work seriously, not myself. I don't have any of those 'artistic' hang-ups, and I have total contempt for them at all times and under all circumstances." A suggestion that acting out some barbarity against a pretend-victim may have offered a relief valve for personal frustrations was met with similar denunciation. "I don't find that acting the heavy is in any way emotionally cathartic," Elam said. "I can't believe that I ever really got anything out of my system by going out there sneerin' 'n' growlin' 'n' firin' the gun. It's work, and it's really not near as hard work being a heavy as doing comedy. Comedy is *four* times as tough, *much* more emotionally draining. Being a heavy, you just sit there and *sneer*, and it's all perfect."

The rich, natural coarseness of Elam's voice added authority to his statements, and sometimes signalled a vexation directed, not at his interviewer personally, but at misconceptions underlying some of the questions. When I erroneously stated his birthplace, he quickly corrected, "I was born in Miami, Arizona, not Phoenix. Miami is a little mining town out in the middle of nowhere. I did grow up in Phoenix and graduated from high school there." I made the assumption that his native background in the Southwest predetermined his placement in Western films, and he retorted, "I don't think that has anything to do with it. At the time I started, they were making lots of Westerns, and my contacts were in the Western field, and I seemed to fit the style of what at that time was the Western heavy."

His perfect alignment with that style over the years makes it difficult now to conceive a smaller, more innocent-looking version of Jack Elam, but I grasped at an image associated with halcyon youth as if to allow him — like the proverbial bum who started out life in a mansion — to utter, "I was not always as you see me now."

"Tell me," I offered, "were you ever a Boy Scout?" I struck a nerve, for a reason he made obvious.

"*Yes*, I was a Boy Scout," he gruffed, "and not happily so. It was at a Boy Scout meeting that I lost the sight of one eye, and it was very poorly handled, that particular incident, by the old Scout department at the time. Even after I had had a pencil run through my eye, I was forced to stand at attention for two hours, for the balance of the meeting, at the risk of, uh ... 'not being a good Scout.' I think that's a lot of bullshit!"

Regrettable as this accident was, it did indirectly effect Elam's passage into films, beginning with *Rawhide* in 1950, and including among his earliest work the classic *High Noon*. Unfortunately the somber overtones of that picture did not require a fuller rendition of Elam's character, and we will never view a scene he described. "I played 'Charlie,'" he recalled. "I'm the one that Gary Cooper kept looking in on at the cell — I was sleeping in jail — and he finally came over and let me out; and I asked if the bars were open, and he says yes, to go ahead. I wandered down the street and into the bar — this was as high noon was imminent. We actually shot a long sequence which is not in the film in case there was a lapse in the gunfight, which of course turned out to be one of the best ever, that they could cut back to me as an alcoholic all alone in the bar where I'm wandering around, you know, tucking people's drinks under my hat and under my arm and having a ball with free whiskey, because everyone else has run out at high noon."

I looked over a list of subsequent movies in which Elam appeared, many that have since lapsed into obscurity. I noted that, at least on the basis of titles, they sounded like a pretty poor run, citing three from 1952 — *Lure of the Wilderness, My Man and I,* and *Rancho Notorious* — released the same year as *High Noon.*

"I'll concede that I've done a lot of second-class pictures. However," he qualified, "those that you mention were not all ... *Lure of the Wilderness* was not a bad picture at *all*. It was a remake of *Swamp Water*. And *My Man and I* was a *sensational* picture! William Wellman directed it. It was with Ricardo Montalban, Shelley Winters ... and as a matter of fact I played a Mexican grape picker, and it was my first comedy role. People think that my comedy came late, but that's not true. Harry Evans, a columnist at the time, even suggested me for an award for that picture. And *Rancho Notorious* was no great shakes, but it was a well done picture, a Fritz Lang Western with Marlene Dietrich; you know, a rather eminent cast."

"...*Gun Belt, Gun Runners*...," I continued down the list.

"Forget it."

"...*Cattle Queen of Montana, Ride Vacquero*..."

"*Ride Vacquero* was a very large, pretentious Western with Robert Taylor."

"Against a backdrop, then, of a quarter-century of working in both major and minor productions, it seems at least that public as well as critical respect for your work is quite high. Perhaps," I suggested, "there's no way of knowing how high it would be had you not been curtailed by some of the second-rate vehicles."

"I've maybe been curtailed by the fact that I didn't get a lot of roles I'd like to have had," he countered, "but *I* don't *feel* that any of my potential's been curtailed by material."

"What was it," I asked, "that casting directors were looking for when choosing villains that they found so frequently in Jack Elam? A face? A physique? An adaptability? Some inherent quality?"

"I would have to say probably just the fact that on film," Elam chopped the sentence's remainder into distinct words, "I ... project ... evil. It worked under all sorts of circumstances. Either frantic evilness, or the quiet villainy—whatever it was, it worked for me. And I don't think physique had anything to do with it. I didn't weigh 140 pounds when I first started. I was at the same height that I am now, six feet, one and a half inches. I was skinny! I didn't have any adaptability. I don't think the fact that my eye I don't see out of doesn't really line up, that wasn't really that noticeable in the early days. As I'm getting older, now, it's beginning to be a little more obvious. But some inherent quality? I'd say, no. Those are the roles they gave me because of my appearance, and I think I was able to sell 'em, and ... that's the whole story."

In obvious contrast to Jack Elam's impressive villains of the fifties, he began in the early sixties gradually to accumulate sympathetic roles, and to exercise a raucous comic style that has become as much a trademark as his heavies. Nineteen sixty-one saw him as an amusing skid row acquaintance of Apple Annie's in *Pocketful of Miracles*. In the Western television series "The Dakotas" of 1962 he portrayed a bounty hunter for a change, rather than a fugitive from the law. Later he went on to *The Way West* as a sanctimonious scamp of a parson in 1967. He showed himself to be a highly workable co-star on the side of James Garner in *Support Your Local Sheriff* (1969), and with John Wayne in *Rio Lobo* (1970). Still, Elam's own recollections were keener than mine regarding these transitions, and he performed the necessary adjustments. "Don Collier wasn't the lawman in 'The Dakotas,'" he corrected me on one point. "He was in another series, I think it was called 'The Lawmen' or something. 'The Dakotas' was with Larry Ward. You mention *Pocketful of Miracles*. I don't really consider that I *did Pocketful of Miracles*. It was such a small, you know, passing-through thing. I frankly don't remember the role. I'm surprised that anybody does. Of course, I did enjoy *Support Your Local Sheriff* ... but I've done comedy off and on over the years, a lo-o-ong time before anybody seems to remember. Like, I did the 'Toothy Thompson' character in two or three series out at 'Bronco' and 'Sugarfoot' for Warner Brothers."

"Before breaking out of the strictly villainous mold, did you ever resent that stereotype," I asked, "and did you welcome the chance to diversify into comedy and serio-comic roles?"

"Well of course," he replied, "but it's not important. I never felt any resentment about being stereotyped as a heavy if the role was good, if I got well compensated for it. Why ... *I* don't have any driving thing inside me about playing *any* particular role. I don't need to do *Hamlet*," he stressed, "to feel that I've *lived*."

While that plum role may forever elude Elam's grasp, in recent years he has not only achieved variety in characters, but stature as a leading man, which raised the question of why he still listed himself in the *Academy Players Directory* (a thick album consulted during the selection of casts for film productions) not as a leading man, but only in the back section with the "Characters." Many actors whose body of work lies entirely within the character setting field purchase ads in the front section as "Leading Men." Others appear in both sections. Did Elam's sole "Character" listing indicate resignation to a permanent niche in supporting parts, with starring roles regarded more as occasional "gravy?"

"About that dual listing in the *Players Directory*, I think that's just wishful thinking, or hopes, or ... I don't know what it is, and I don't care. I don't think the fact that you list yourself under 'Characters' necessarily means that you are *resigned* to some kind of minor niche. I've had pictures come out lately," he said, "*The Winds of Autumn* and *The Creature from Black Lake*, both of which I have top billing as the top star, and in neither of them am I a conventional leading man. In each case, it's a character role. So I don't see that there's any 'resignation' or anything to not thinking of myself as a leading man."

"Considering for a moment 'the road not taken'," I pursued, "have you ever contemplated where you would be today if you were picked up not as a character actor, but as a romantic lead?"

"I do not suffer from any wanting to be a romantic lead," Elam said. "However, you know, strangely enough I've done many *guest* romantic roles, where there was a romance between me and somebody else in the show. Always on the side of pathos, or whatever; but in many cases, very attractive women have become my spouse or enamorata."

Since Elam had been, after all, a supporting actor for most of his career, and even the films in which he shared or held the central role were hardly blockbusters, I presented from these facts a couple of extrapolations: His income, no doubt, had always fallen far short of Hollywood's major stars'. On the other hand, his own salary as a Hollywood actor exceeded the national average by a tidy sum, putting him in touch with all the frills that lesser mortals generally associate with "Tinseltown"—economic power, stables of cars, the ability to travel at will, to accumulate parcels of real estate, to immensely improve one's circumstances. Asked if his proportionally lower pay bracket had ever made him bitter, Elam snorted, "Definitely not! I think with some pictures I've done, I felt that I would have liked to have been paid more; but at the time, my stature didn't *warrant* a higher salary. I don't see how I can complain. I drive a Cadillac, which I own. My wife has a Mark IV, which we own. We live in a very lovely home. We have an acre of gardens and a pool. How the hell can I complain?" He refuted the second assumption, saying, "I don't consider that I have *any* kind of 'economic power.' It's been a very lucrative profession for me, so I have economic *success*. I've travelled a lot, as you indicate. Self-betterment...? I don't know. I question that. I think an auditor is just as well equipped for self-betterment as an actor.

"But I do have the time now, and the money, that I can enjoy my *family* more. Actually, the more successful I get, the more I turn back inside to the family and exclude outside matters. You don't *need* them. Now, instead of travelling alone, if I do have to travel on location ... why, the family goes and we enjoy each other's company."

"Has your career—the money, anything—changed you in any way?"

"I don't know that it's changed me at all," he laughed, "except that I take it a lot easier now than I used to. I don't have any, you know, great hang-ups that I can think of."

One more fringe benefit of actors came to mind: access to the open forum, a closeness to the media from which various causes are hailed and bandwagons roll forth. "And what," I asked, "has your career allowed you to contribute to others?" His answer revealed a surprising, but very respectable form of philanthropy.

"Well," Elam replied, "I don't have to push anybody around. And I don't step on anybody. And I mind my own business. I'll settle for that contribution from anybody else in the world."

"Let's talk about the changes that have taken place in movies since you began acting," I said. "You played 'Alamosa Bill' in Sam Peckinpah's *Pat Garrett & Billy the Kid*, and I think your scene with Kris Kristofferson as 'Billy' says a lot about the turn that pictures in general have taken lately, particularly those that have de-romanticized the Old West. For example, 'Alamosa Bill' is an aging lawman who, as a competent peace officer, has pretty much played out his string. He's a little edgy, and too scared to play fair in a step-off duel with the Kid. 'Bill' turns on the count of 'nine,' but 'Billy' turned on the count of 'one' and survived by being a better cheater."

Elam dismissed my analogy, saying, "I don't see that as any particular similarity to the direction films have taken. I don't think necessarily anything that happens in a Peckinpah picture has any relationship to the rest of film making. It's something *he* does, ideas and creations of his *own*."

"But did you feel a little out of your element in *Pat Garrett & Billy the Kid*; or do you consider the more graphic displays of sex and violence that have come to characterize American film of the last decade to be healthy developments?"

"Well, you see," he answered, "I don't find any *good* developments in the Western field at all. You tell me you can gross umpteen-million dollars with a gross, insulting thing like *Blazing Saddles* ... *that's* not a Western!" he grumbled. "It makes *fun* of Westerns! I don't see any healthy aspect to the Western field at all today. Unfortunately, it's fa-a-ar removed from the old days."

"How is that?"

"I don't think they really write any more 'black' heavies to play against the 'white' hero, and I think that's unfortunate; because, you know, they've got a lot of, uh ... 'gray' heavies who are semisympathetic, and that's kind of a *bore* to me. I liked the way we did it for twenty-five years, where the heavy was a heavy because he wanted the money or the cattle or ... or he was just a plain sonovabitch!"

"How did you go about putting that kind of role across?" I asked. "Was there ever a special drive behind your many evil characterizations? I think what I'm getting at is something a 'method' actor would call 'motivation.' Did you ever have a chance to inject a personal philosophy or a view of evil into a role?"

In the same way Elam denied that playing the heavy was a useful emotional outlet, he nixed this idea, too. "There has been *no* special drive behind any of my so-called evil portrayals. I just do the role, and I do not try to inject any personal philosophy or 'view of evil' into any of my roles. I think I do in some of the comedy. I try to get in some of my feelings... Like in 'The Texas Wheelers,' I was trying to implant a lot of things, ideas, or just an attitude that I am familiar with."

"The Texas Wheelers," a quickly axed comedy series where Elam starred as a blustery ne'er-do-well returning to the family he had abandoned, premiered on ABC during that network's last year in the ratings basement. It was an opportunity richly deserved by Elam, and had it appeared in the following season when ABC shot to the top, Elam may still have been a weekly television delight. On "'The Texas Wheelers'," Elam reflected, "I *loved* the show, and I'm *much* more sorry than anybody that it didn't last. And I'm really sorry it never got a full run. Nobody ever saw enough of 'em to find out whether or not they'd like it. I thought it was a sure thing. Its failure was not only a disappointment. It was *ab*-solutely unbelievable to me." I mentioned some of his subsequent television ventures, singling out in particular his wino-in-the-park, a recurrent foil for Cloris Leachman. "I do not enjoy the television cameos like that one in 'Phyllis'," he replied, "even though it seems to have worked all right. It's a lot more work for me to go into another medium. You see, that's a live show, and you work before an audience, and that's not my gig at all."

"Television doesn't seem to be a medium that's generated a lot of happiness for you. I don't suppose you look forward to ever getting involved with a series again."

"I would like very much to think so," Elam answered cheerfully. "There's constantly new series being suggested to me, and we talk about them and I read scripts. I wouldn't mind being tied into a series, if it's the right role and it's lucrative enough. I mean, I think it's a very nice way to live.

"I've travelled so much in films," he explained. "All the pictures I do, I have to be *gone* for. I'm a little tired of travelling, and I'd be very happy to stay home and do a series."

In addition to the travel, the many weeks spent on location that understandably have wearied Elam, was there another burden unique to his status in Hollywood? What was the fan-on-the-street's reaction on meeting him? Had his tough-guy image ever posed a problem out in public? "It has posed *no* problems of any kind," he said. "People don't try to pick fights with me... I mean, an actor has the same amount of trouble that anybody has, and for the same reasons." Since his roles have mellowed in recent years, I asked if the public now regarded him differently. "The public response hasn't changed. Strangely enough, the only thing my career has done, the more you work and the longer you've been around, the more you are recognized in public. But the people I see today — even though they see me and say, 'Oh! We saw you in "The Texas Wheelers"!' — they still think of me... Their reaction is, 'Boy! *You're* the *heavy*!' They don't let go of that fact, that I began as a heavy and did nothing but heavies practically for so many years.

"I still get in one now and then. I like it. I did *The Winds of Autumn* not long ago in which I was an out-and-out, total, thoroughbred heavy; and I like to keep that alive because that's... — " his voice trailed off for a second as if he couldn't quite comprehend it — "somehow, that image has never left the public."

Elam's wonderment, his seeming unawareness of his own impact on film, was disarming; but it served to reveal one other handicap known to many professional actors. One can only guess that it is almost the devil's dues, the price they pay for all the eyes that fall on them. Apparently not even Elam — with his informal background in acting and completely unpresumptuous approach to it — is exempted. The price: Actors, being the originators of a drama and living it from the inside, cannot freshly experience its terrors and delights in detachment, from the outside as we can.

For the grizzled veteran, Hollywood's Villain Emeritus, there remained only one more prepared question. What did he think was his best piece of work?

"I don't know that I would be in a position to judge it. If I had to really pick one, I'd probably pick an obscure little TV movie for ABC called *The Cock-Eyed Cowboys of Calico County*. I don't think I'll ever get any better than that. And I don't think there was anything wrong with *Support Your Local Sheriff*. I'm also proud of 'The Texas Wheelers' series, and a great number of 'The Dakotas.' I think they were very acceptable; whereas, like in *Baby Face Nelson* I won the French Palms Award back in the late fifties, and I don't consider that any great piece of work at all."

It could be said, indeed, that Jack Elam was crusty. That crust was decorous, helpful, but — not to be taken personally — quarrelsome. For him, it seemed, to allow minor factual errors to stand was pointless as long as there was a chance to rectify them; but even more intolerable were the slanderous exaggerations — as he saw them — about actors and acting engendered by the many pretensions of Hollywood, and these he had tilted his lance against with a vengeance.

Here also was the warm family man, the private man, and a traditionalist who cherished some of the old ways, because he knew a simple hero/villain formula — in the hands of a Gary Cooper, a Robert Taylor, or some of the other greats he had battled on screen — could come across with force and dignity. It seemed only fair that I hand him a free rein before I let him go. Was there anything, I asked, anything he would like to say about himself that hadn't been covered by a question? Once again, I hit crust.

"That's a tempting offer," he rasped. There was a gravelly laugh, the kind that used to come from Jack Elam the rustler, Elam the bully, Elam the bushwacker. "I can just say I like cigars, Cutty Sark, and a good poker game." It was not difficult to picture him leaning forward through a swirl of cheroot smoke to tap my notepad with a long trigger finger. Piercing that infernal haze I could fancy the famous glint, the twisted smile as he added in a rumbling voice, "And *don't* ever put down that I said," (in a singsong) "'I-I-I-I li-i-ike pe-e-eople' ... because I rarely meet a man that lives up to his billing." [April 1976.]

Not overly tall, but square-shouldered and rock solid. Hair disheveled in angry spikes. A toothy jack-o'-lantern leer. Bullying Anthony Perkins as *The Tin Star*'s greenhorn sheriff, and leading a lynch mob against him; or in *Cry Terror*, attempting to rape Inger Stevens who, in desperation, breaks a picture frame and guts him with a shard of glass. Playing cutthroat renegade Indians, or Al Capone for television's "The Untouchables." A deep, coarse, no-nonsense voice. A sensationally vivid, bristly toughness. These recollections are practically automatic, and they did not quite jibe with a wirephoto showing hair combed flat, a fresh shave, a placid grin, a clean, Western style shirt, and a caption reading: "In Satisfactory Condition."

In an Associated Press news brief dated December 9, 1978, L.A. County Fire Capt. John Everett gave credit to 16-year-old Brian Gonzalez for pulling Neville Brand to safety from his burning Malibu home. A year later I was able to call Brand and learn particulars of his accident first-hand. "I was trying to save my books," Brand told me, "but I stayed in there too long, and ... it happened."

"Business books," I anticipated, that being a reasonable excuse for taking the risk that he did.

"No," he said, "not business books at all."

"Rare books, then," I said. "First editions."

"Some of them were, yes, but I'm not a rare book collector. I collect books, read a lot," he stated. "I had about 30,000 I'd collected over the past thirty years, and I was trying to save them. Saved a *lot*."

Brand's brush with death in Malibu had hardly been the first in his life, nor the closest. Hoping to follow a military precedent set by his father, a Signal Corpsman during World War I, Brand graduated from high school and, still six months short of legal age, joined the Army with the elder Brand's signed consent. As it so happened, he came to distinguish himself in combat on some of the same battlefronts seen by his father in the earlier conflict. "According to one film reference," I mentioned to Brand in raising this subject, "you were the fourth most decorated American soldier of World War II."

"Well, that's not true," he replied, flattered by the inaccuracy, but unwilling to usurp that position from its rightful holder, whoever it was. "What happened is, I'm way up there, I'm one of the tops. But when I got to Hollywood here, it started out at whatever it was — eighth, or whatever — then some guy'd pick it up, and before you know, I'm way up higher. Then when I'd deny it, they thought I was just being modest. So, I just let it go. That's something that happens over the years, you know.

"Yeah," Brand owned, "I got quite a war experience. I went Regular Army during peacetime. I was in, oh, maybe a year, and then war broke out in Europe. They broke us up into cadres and sent me to Colorado Springs. I trained there, became a platoon sergeant, and wound up in Europe with the First Army, 89th Division. Jeeze, I got the Silver Star, the Bronze Star, a whole *pile* of medals."

"You spent ten years in the Army," I said, consulting the same flawed reference. "That was half a career, right there. Why didn't you finish it out?"

"It was nine years," Brand made another correction. "Well, yeah, that's why I went in. I was gonna be a professional soldier — you know, a twenty year man — but by the time the war ended ... I'd had it. I was in a hospital in Nancy, France, when it was over. The last time I got hit was about three weeks before the Germans surrendered. When it ended, we all knew it was over, and it pissed me off because here I was. I couldn't make it to the very end.

"When I got hit, I was somewhere up near the Elbe River, just about as far as the Americans went. We had those bastards all surrounded in pockets. They started drivin' around in our equipment they'd captured; and German jeeps and things had the Allied white star painted on 'em. They'd been pullin' that trick before, in the Bulge. So the company commander sent me down with a couple of my scouts into a village off one of those big goddamn Hitler autobahns to see whether it was Germans or Americans there ... and I got down too far, and it was Germans. They opened up on us, and they had us — in the back, in the front — we couldn't get out. It took a whole battalion to get three guys out. We were all hit .. but they got us out.

"Yeah, I was a crazy kid, like we all were," he said, a little distantly. "I couldn't do it again. You only do that kind of thing once."

"Regrets?"

"Oh no," he responded quickly. "I have no regrets. But it was a different world then. I wouldn't know what the hell I was fighting for, if it was today. I really wouldn't. Everything was pretty simple in those days, as you remember. You knew where you were at, and you were backed full to the hilt, and morale was very high. You didn't have any of that Vietnam problem that those guys had, with all those desertions, and morale was very low. It was a different war, back then. It was a different country, it was different men. A different *breed* of men then, from the young kids today. It was a different ... everything."

"Have you ever gone back over the old invasion route, maybe with a picture on location?"

"No," Brand said, it seemed, with cool disinterest. "I got awful close on this one I did last year. I was over there on an American film for six months in Budapest, Hungary, then we shot part of it in Vienna. Some of the boys that weren't working went into Munich, and I had a chance to, but I didn't. I'd been around there before. After the war, I was in the Army of Occupation, and they trucked us to Hitler's home in Berchtesgaden, took us on a tour of the whole goddamn place."

"Do hostile memories survive?" I probed, misreading a bitterness in his words. "Did you not go because of holdover feelings from the war, a hatchet that won't stay buried? With all your experiences, I suppose it would be understandable."

"Oh, I never had a hatchet to *start* with," Brand countered. "If there was ever any animosity at all, in *my* outfit, it was at the people back home. I remember once during the Belgian Bulge, we get a *Stars & Stripes* and read in a headline that John L. Lewis had called a coal strike. *We were freezing fucking to death!* And we were out of ammunition ... we were losing the *war*. And *that* pissed us off. Things like that.

"But I never did dislike the Germans, even during the war. The regular German soldier in the Wehrmacht — other than the SS — they were clean fighters. We had nothing to do with the SS troops much. They didn't throw 'em in, really, until the end of the war. Now *they* were dirty bastards. We got to see *their* handiwork when we liberated a couple of concentration camps. But the regular German soldier, he was a good soldier, a good fighter, a brave man, and there was no way you could hate 'im. You might hate the government, and you could hate Hitler and all that shit, but you couldn't hate the soldier. They were freezing to death like we were, and they were getting killed like we were. There's a kind of thing that grows up between the two sides, when you're there."

"To come through the war as you did, it seems you had to be made of rather stern stuff to begin with. Were you a pretty tough kid?" I asked.

"I was just one of the guys," Brand said modestly. "I loved sports, played on the teams, but nothing outstanding. I was never a star at it. I was born seventy miles west of Chicago in Kewanee, Illinois, and I did grow up in a tough neighborhood. A 'wrong side of the tracks' sort of thing. It was mostly Slavs, Lithuanians and Poles. Also some Belgians, like us. My three brothers, two sisters and me are Welsh on our mother's side, Belgian–Dutch on our father's. But where we were, it was mostly steelworkers, or laborers on the Kewanee Board of Works. And you *had* to fight in my neighborhood. I can't remember ever not fighting as a kid, and to me it was very natural. The first thing you learned was how to fight. If you couldn't, you didn't live long."

"So how was it you came to follow the acting Muse?"

"I haven't the slightest idea," Brand chuckled. "I didn't know what I was doing, I just did it. After I got out of the Army, I went to drama school on the GI Bill at the American Theater Wing in New York. I stayed in school for three-and-a-half years, but I started working professionally in less than a year. While I was still in school I came out to Hollywood and was doing small roles in pictures. In 1949 I did my first one, *Port of New York*, which starred Yul Brynner; and then *D.O.A.*"

"So many actors have had to go for years without their first paying job," I said. "Do you have any idea why you took off so quickly?"

"No, I really don't. I imagine that, at the time, there was just nobody around that was like me. I didn't look like anybody else, my style of work was a little different. I think that had something to do with it. I was also working my ass off in New York, I was doing plays, and I was becoming a very good actor. Then you do a few good jobs in pictures, and then ... other than that, I don't know. I just don't."

"Did they have you doing straight heavies right out of the gate?"

Jack Elam in a publicity shot from the early fifties.   25

Opposite: **Strother Martin**, Ernest Borgnine, **Jack Elam** as three badmen pursued by Raquel Welch in *Hannie Caulder*, 1971. Above: As a safety conscious deputy, **Elam** (right) arrives, late as usual, on the action in *Support Your Local Sheriff*, 1969. James Garner wields gun, Tom Reese sprawls.

 Jack Elam is a man who likes a good cigar…

Top: **Neville Brand** (center) faces Rory Calhoun's gun in *Raw Edge*, 1956; Rex Reason (far left) and Emile Meyer look less worried than they ought. Bottom: **Brand** badgers Anthony Perkins, a greenhorn marshal in *The Tin Star*, 1957.

Opposite, top: **Neville Brand** (left) and Frank Gorshin play dirty for Walt Disney in *That Darn Cat*, 1964. Bottom: Inger Stevens is cornered by **Brand** in *Cry Terror*, 1958. Above: **Brand** in *The Deadly Trackers*, 1973.

32   **A fresh-faced Lee Van Cleef** from the early fifties.

Top: **Lee Van Cleef** (abed) and Stephen Boyd scheme, Albert Salmi dreams, and Henry Silva steams in *The Bravados*, 1958. Bottom: Lee Marvin trips "Pilgrim" James Stewart to the bemusement of **Van Cleef** and **Strother Martin** in *The Man Who Shot Liberty Valance*, 1962.

Opposite, top: **Lee Van Cleef** as Col. Mortimer (left) retrieves his gun from "The Man with No Name" (Clint Eastwood) after killing "El Indio" (Gian Maria Volonte) in *For a Few Dollars More*, 1966. Bottom: **Van Cleef** picks an easy target, Gianpiero Albertini, in *Sabata*, 1969. Above: "Angel Eyes" **Van Cleef**, one of the unholy three of *The Good, the Bad, and the Ugly*, 1967.

Opposite: **Luke Askew** as a hired gun earning his keep with *The Culpepper Cattle Company*, 1972. Above, top: **Askew**, the enigmatic hitchhiker, parts company with "Captain America," Peter Fonda, in *Easy Rider*, 1969. Bottom: **Askew** and Jorge Russek, as friends of William Bonnie, regard lawman James Coburn with suspicion in *Pat Garrett and Billy the Kid*, 1973.

Opposite: Sarah Miles comforts **Bo Hopkins,** her defender, in *The Man Who Loved Cat Dancing*, 1973. Above: **Hopkins** in costume for *American Graffiti*, 1973.

Top: **Bo Hopkins** reasons against nonviolence with Gary Grimes in *The Culpepper Cattle Company*, 1972. Bottom: Police brutality Texas style: Timothy Bottoms is shoved by sheriff **Hopkins** toward a copse, to be worked over, in *A Small Town in Texas*, 1976.

"Not in New York. In the theater, there's no such thing as typecasting. In classroom work, especially, you do everything; scenes from plays, all the classics. In the regular work, however, I did mostly contemporary pieces. The last one I did, which I liked, was about eight years ago. It was for Sidney Kingsley called *Mainline*, a takeoff on Jimmy Hoffa.

"But I left the theater. I wasn't really in it too long. I never really got to be what you'd call a man who fell in love with the theater. I was trained in it, and that's about it. There's so much about it that didn't appeal to me, playing that same role over and over. I don't have that kind of patience. With a film, you go in, you do it, it's over, and you go on to other things, or go fishing or hunting someplace. I have more fun making pictures, and the life suits me much better.

"In the beginning, in pictures," he recounted, "I played a few soldiers — like in *The Halls of Montezuma* — and *then* I got into heavies, and they had me doing that for a long time. So I played the villain, playing mostly either heavies or neurotics — *real* heavy shit! Heavy toads. Real dramatic. When you're first starting, it's good to be typed. It really is, because you get into that groove and it gets you work. Much later on you can go in for variety. But I was never getting any light stuff, and never any comedy, ever. A couple of times I just packed up and went back to New York. I'd had it. And then I started to turn down a lot.

"I think that what broke me out of doing heavies was when I did the series 'Laredo,' and that was a comedy. Nobody had thought I could *do* comedy, and there I was playing comedy every week in a series. *That* changed the whole picture. People could see that my range was very wide, and that I could do almost anything. After that, I just started to do *everything*. I haven't been typed now for the last ten years."

"As a villain, there's no telling how many fight scenes you did. I remember one in a Rory Calhoun Western," I said, "perhaps it was *Raw Edge*, in which you and one of the other heavies were having it out. He put you out of commission — temporarily, at least — by slamming you in the head with an empty coal scuttle. Did you ever get hurt in any of these tussles?"

"Oh *yeah*," Brand declared, "*many* times! And I've been hurt workin' around horses too, you know. I've been thrown from horses, I've broken ribs. Oh, Christ yes! But that's all part of it. You just pick yourself up and go forward."

"In playing one of those fight scenes or something equally stirring — which, goodness knows, you've done plenty of — do *you* get caught up in it emotionally, as so many actors claim to do?" I asked.

"You can get launched into a scene, and go quite a ways with it, yeah," he admitted, "but another part of you is controlling it. If you go *all* the way with it, you're not controlling it. There's a part of you that has to be very cool."

"What about playing the villain? Does it take a special approach?"

"Well, no. Not at all, because I don't go in thinking he's a villain. The audience might, but the *villain* doesn't think he's a villain. It's the same story when you're playing comedy. The audience is laughing, but *you* don't think, at the time, that what you're doing is funny," Brand pointed out. "So, nobody thinks he's a villain. Even a *killer* condones what he's done. I just create this human being under the circumstances that are given. I don't think he's a villain or, if I'm doing something else, that he's a 'good guy.' We don't think of *ourselves* that way. We don't say, 'I'm a good guy.' Everybody just condones his own actions."

"What kind of effect did it have on your children, your being an actor, and one of Hollywood's most eminent screen heavies?"

"Well," Brand considered, "the latter part doesn't apply so much, because these are brand new children. One's only twenty and the other's twenty-two. Here in Malibu, though, it's loaded with actors, I've taken them on location when there was a chance, so they've grown right with it. It was never a big deal, because they've always been in the middle of it. In fact, Michele, my twenty-two-year-old, is studying in San Francisco at the conservatory now." He added with fatherly pride, but in tones of knock-on-wood, "She wants to be an actress, and she looks ... promising."

"Do you worry that it will be tougher for Michele to break in than it was for you?"

"No, I don't think it will. In certain ways, it's easier. When I came into the business, it was just theater and films. Now there's television, with *thousands* of jobs for actors."

"What kind of reaction have you gotten from the public in response to the rugged image you've had to project over the years, even in sympathetic roles?" I asked.

"Oh, I get very *good* reactions, *very* good vibes from the public," Brand replied. "It's *always* been that way, with people from all walks of life. And especially from minority groups — Mexicans, blacks — people like that. I think it's because I've always played the guy against authority, the heavy ... and this is their side. They can identify with that."

"That image of toughness is awfully hard to dismiss," I insisted. "Even in a likable character, such as the turnkey in *Birdman of Alcatraz* where we watched you and Burt Lancaster grow old together and come to respect one another, or in the half-breed scout with John Wayne in *Cahill, U.S. Marshal*, there is always that forbidding quality. It causes anyone to wonder, Mr. Brand, where the character ends and the real man begins, or where they are the same. Do you think there are any misconceptions about you, personally, that you'd like to clear up?"

"Well, where the two things come together and where they differ," Brand stated frankly, "you never know. That's something you can never ever define. You don't know where it ends and where it overlaps, but it's there.

"I don't think people have any *misconceptions*, however, if they see enough of you on screen, and if you're a good actor. See, a *bad* actor you can never get to know, never — because he's *acting*. But a good actor, if you've watched 'im in a number of roles... Just like a good writer, if you read three or four of his books, you get to know the man pretty well. He comes through. *He* does. So people that have seen me, not just in one role, but in several roles — see the comedy, like 'Laredo,' and then see Capone, and then see something else — they won't *have* any misconceptions, because a lot of myself comes through. What they see there underneath those roles is what I am, you see?

"It's *not* a 'tough guy.' It's ... it's a *rough* guy, let's put it that way. *Not* 'tough.' But it's a man who was a sergeant in World War II, who led men all through the war. It's a man who has lived all of his life outdoors. I read a lot. I live right on the edge of the sea, here in Malibu, so I do most of the water stuff. A guy who's been around animals. I've been around horses, I'm a good rider. I understand animals, I've tracked them. I've fished for marlin. I used to own a sailboat — I don't at the moment now — but I sail this Pacific Ocean out here, all alone ... and that's the kind of life I live.

"But a tough guy? No, I am not a tough guy... *But*, I can *do* all those things. Like in the war, I can fight and get through anything, *rough* it through. I try not to be a tough guy, not in my personal life — but I *can* be, if the situation calls for it." [November 1979.]

Vintage 1952, Black-and-White.

Long Shot: A ridgetop cluster of gnarled trees.

Medium Shot: A cowboy is perched on a rock in quarter-right profile, studiously dragging on the butt of a roll-your-own.

Close-up: He moves forward. The sheen of sweat, a three-day-old five o'clock shadow, the intent stare the cowboy gives a rider galloping toward him across a tree-dotted slope, and the soundtrack's dull, cardiac thump on the back of a guitar all reek with the import that this man is up to no good.

Thus *High Noon* opened on a note of threat, dwelling on the sharp, menacing features and pantherly swagger of Lee Van Cleef who, when called for, subsequently never failed to look the part of a villain. In movies and television his narrowed hazel eyes darted shiftily for dozens of scheming rats, and cornered outlaws about to make a desperate stand. The most galling bullies and blackhearted killers wore his toothy leer. Even on occasional furlough from the cowboy heavy, he always manifested a restive toughness; as a soldier, for example, in *The Beast from 20,000 Fathoms*. Playing a sharpshooter picked to bring down the tyrannosaurus, he curtly grunted when asked if he could fire a grenade rifle, "I can pick my teeth with it." Very tough. Primarily, though, Van

Cleef's stock in trade for roughly 13 years was supportive acting as a bad-man in Westerns, gracing some of the finest made in that span: *The Tin Star*, *Gunfight at the OK Corral*, *The Bravados*, and *The Man Who Shot Liberty Valance*. It all began with the classic *High Noon* wherein—perhaps of interest only to trivia buffs and the superstitious—for his very first role, he was listed 13th in the credits.

Lee Van Cleef advanced rapidly from Hollywood character actor to international star by way of the "spaghetti Western." That term, not coined in flattery, unjustly belittles what it labels. For years, Continental producers had capitalized on the popularity of various American actors, putting one at the head of a European cast in a low-budget suspense or action feature, and releasing the product to European exhibitors. It was a modestly lucrative formula. It was not expected, however, to concoct a runaway box office hit from one particular 1965 Western opus, and to open the American market for a glut of good and bad imitations. "Westerns" had been produced in Europe before, but none like *Per un Pugno di Dollari*, filmed the previous year in Spain on Italian, German and Spanish monies by Italian director Sergio Leone. For its lead he had hired an American TV actor, Clint Eastwood (not his first choice), for a flat $15,000. The 96-minute feature—in English, *A Fistful of Dollars*—made its scruffy antihero, "The Man with No Name," so popular, Leone devised a two hour, ten minute sequel, *Per Qualche Dollaro in Più*, on a half-million dollar budget, shot in Spain as well; and capped the series with his sprawling (two hours, 41 minutes) *Il Buono, il Bruto, il Cattivo*. A copyright suit from the Japanese makers of *Yojimbo* alleged that *A Fistful of Dollars'* plot had been pirated from their Samurai tale, and held up its American release. Confident in the drawing power of his creations, Leone at last issued *Fistful* to American theaters in 1967. Its sequels, *For a Few Dollars More* and *The Good, the Bad, and the Ugly*, followed in 1967 and 1968, and garnered $10 million dollars apiece in the U.S. and Italy alone.

The look of Leone's American West was utterly novel. Compared especially to most contemporaneous television offerings, there were no well-tailored, carefully barbered leading men, no shiny-tressed lovelies, no California beachboy extras. Leone peopled his films with a coarse-looking, often ugly crowd. The "Dollars" trilogy assembled men and women whose garments, whose very persons appeared weathered and grimy, as they could not have looked otherwise in a frontier environment. He interspersed the standard issue Winchester rifles and Colt peacemakers, so omnipresent in Hollywood Westerns, among a wider array of period firearms. To submerge viewers deeper into observed conflicts, Leone's microphones zoomed in, magnified every breath, every rattle and wheeze of characters facing pain or death, every fly on the wing in stagnant airspace. But to counterweight this almost abrasive realism, the rugged beauty of his "Western" landscapes were captured in vivid color; and breathtaking musical scores by Ennio Morricone intensified the action on screen. Andean flutes, thrumming Spanish guitars, a jaunty mixed chorus, an impudent jew's-harp, a clanging knell, a muted bugle, or a woman's pure-voiced plaint injected excitement, humor or pathos into scenes that built to a crescendo of gunfire, saluted the hero's triumph, or laid bare the wastage of war. While one might have criticized the works for their obviously over-dubbed dialogue, the lip-sync was no more distracting than in more "acceptable" foreign films, and subtitles would have ruined Leone's rather persuasive Old West illusion.

So different was *A Fistful of Dollars* that TIME lauded: "Once in a great while a western comes along that breaks new ground and becomes a classic of the genre.... This year, *A Fistful of Dollars* is the feature that dares to be different."

The level of violence in Leone's pictures created enemies quickly among the critics. TIME called *For a Few Dollars More* "Western Grand Guignol." Regarding *The Good, the Bad, and the Ugly*, Arthur Knight in *Saturday Review* said, "Crammed with sadism and a distaste for human values that would make the ordinary misanthrope seem like Pollyanna, their only possible excuse for existence is that [movies such as this] make money. Somehow, that isn't enough." Of the same film, Renata Adler in the *New York Times* opined, "Zane Grey meets the Marquis de Sade.... It must be the most expensive, pious and repelling movie in the history of its particular genre." The spaghetti Western's eventual relegation to pariah status as film was foreshadowed by a later remark in Adler's review of *The Good, the Bad...*: "Eli Wallach ... is ... once so severely beaten by Van Cleef that anyone who would voluntarily remain in the theater beyond this scene (while he might be a mild, sweet person in his private life) is not someone I should care to meet, in any capacity, ever."

Into this disputed arena stepped Lee Van Cleef in 1965 at Sergio Leone's invitation. He was hired to play ex-Confederate "Col. Mortimer, best shot in the Carolinas," a bounty hunter in *For a Few Dollars More*. The film was Van Cleef's Rubicon. He proved himself worthy of leading roles and sympathetic parts thereafter by a performance which, in one stroke, overturned his long established image as expendable dastard. "Mortimer" cut a magisterial figure; suited and cloaked in black, seen astride a prancing ebony stallion, augustly reading his Bible and puffing on a meerschaum pipe, peering analytically at a new face or an old situation, or cracking a grin that was genial to friend but chilling to foe. A hero's mantle fell so naturally onto Van Cleef's shoulders in *For a Few Dollars More*, one could have reasonably asked at the time why this had not happened sooner.

So treacherous was the scramble for buried gold in the next "Dollars" feature, it might have been called—had the parallel occurred to Leone—*It's a Bad, Bad, Bad, Bad World*. With *The Good, the Bad, and the Ugly* it was back to villainy for Lee Van Cleef, but this time as a title character (unquestionably *Bad*), essentially coequal with Clint Eastwood

(*Good*) and Eli Wallach (*Ugly*). Again he carried a prime role with élan as the cruel "Setenza" or, as he was better known, "Angel Eyes." The three protagonists were sweethearts not a one. Each contributed his share to the film's high body count. Still, "Blondie" (Eastwood) confined his shooting to wanted men and self-defense; and "Tuco" (Wallach) to fellow criminals who crossed him. "Angel Eyes," a whored gun, would kill anybody for money or fun.

In retrospect, the segment introducing him at the film's beginning captures "Angel Eyes" in a nutshell. That footage also exemplifies Van Cleef's strong presence as actor/villain, and the maligned spaghetti Western's ability to enchant its audience with taut direction, haunting music, austere landscapes, detailed period settings, and manifested extremes of human terror and brutishness.

"Angel Eyes" rode into a farmstead, dismounted, and joined a former partner in crime at his dinner table. A corrupt general had hired "Angel Eyes" to interrogate the man on the whereabouts of a stolen payroll, then to dispose of him; an assignment "Angel Eyes" coolly laid out to his old friend as they ate together. The man nervously consumed his last meal, paid "Angel Eyes" to avenge his own execution, and manfully went for his gun. "Angel Eyes'" bullet smashed up through the table and dinner plates, and squarely into its mark. The assassin scooped up his new commission, killed his host's two loyal sons, and left his widow weeping in a scene of Old Testament spoil. He returned to the general, waking him in his dark hovel to supply the requested intelligence, collected his pay, and fulfilled his new contract without an ounce of regret by drilling the seedy old coot through a pillow; not so much to muffle the sound of his gun as to see feathers fly ... "the bad."

Ultimately director Sergio Solima awarded Van Cleef his first unshared lead with *La Resa dei Conti* (*The Big Gundown*). He redeemed himself as a sympathetic character of the antiheroic strain, prompting film historian James Robert Parish to this compliment: "Van Cleef as Jonathan Corbett ... presents a far more realistic picture of the western good/badman than does Eastwood's 'Man With No Name' ... more in the starkly realistic tradition of the cowboy genre (as per William S. Hart)." With Clint Eastwood's departure for Hollywood, Van Cleef succeeded him as most popular star of European Westerns, and a steady output of rugged characterizations sustained him in that position in the coming years. *Gundown* was followed by *Day of Anger*. Later came, among others, *Death Rides a Horse*, *Sabata* (like "Mortimer," another enigmatic, black-clad eminence), *Return of Sabata*, *El Condor*, and *Take a Hard Ride*. His coup abroad opened the way for home based productions of *The Magnificent Seven Ride*, and then *Barquero*, in which he played a brawny, shirtless ferryman who pulled his barge crossriver hand-over-hand, without assist from steam power or beast. More recent assignments have located him in Hong Kong for Run-Run Shaw's *The Stranger and the*

Gunfighter, and home again for a television series pilot, *Escape to Nowhere*, on the Federal witness protection service.

As the foregoing should justify, the fantasy realm of cinema could crown Lee Van Cleef its Darkling Prince of the West. Teeming rabble would cheer this elevation, having laid down a mountain of farthings in willing tribute. Meanwhile, pockets of blue-blooded clerisy would scowl, tilt against him with quills that swished furiously in the air like the tails of so many belligerent lapdogs, and dispatch throughout the kingdom their protests at his "usurpation."

For the real counterparts of these opposing factions, Van Cleef's critics and fans, his own words should be instructive. Too much footage projects him as the tough bareknuckles fighter and deadly gunman for that basis of renown to be denied, but his deposition on the matter as we spoke by telephone one evening provides a more moderate perspective.

I raised the subject of his career as a top-notch heavy, and learned surprisingly that Lee Van Cleef did not view his body of work as a series of violent spectacles. I suggested his naval service in both theaters of World War II undoubtedly offered numerous models for some of his screen roles and ordeals. Rather than his films' being an extension of combat experience, however, he categorized them primarily as outdoor adventures. "I think perhaps the only resource that I've got," he said of preparatory groundwork, "goes back to my childhood, because most of the films that I do are of an outdoor nature. And I was *raised* in the outdoors. I went on my first canoe trip when I was two years old. My dad and mother took me up the Raritan River, and I'm squattin' in the middle of a canoe. I can still remember that. Since then, I went to camps and all those things that a guy goes through in childhood. I was a Boy Scout. I didn't make Eagle, because I was too busy doing swimming, lifesaving and archery, things of that nature, and training other guys in the same area instead of paying attention to my own advancement.

"But I never got out of the woods, in a manner of speaking. I worked on farms after the war. One of the first jobs I had when I got out of the Navy was working in a hunting and fishing camp up in Maine, trying to get it ready for their season. I've always been outside, so *that's* got a *helluva* lot to do with it."

"So your background in Somerville, New Jersey, where you were born, was farming?" I asked.

"Farming? Yes, but when my three kids started coming into the world, my first wife and I just didn't have enough money, so I had to go working where more money was than on a farm. So I went to work in a plant, believe it or not, as a time study methods and motions analyst. I'd never said I'd work indoors in my life. I swore I *wouldn't*, but I *did*."

"How did you become an actor?"

"Accidental!" Van Cleef chuckled. "There was a guy there that said come on out to the country in Clinton, New Jersey, which is kind of the home of little theater. So I went out there with 'im one night and tried out for a part — and damn if I didn't make it! And that thing was 'George' in *Our Town*. And the second one I did out there was 'Joe Pendleton,' the boxer in *Heaven Can Wait*. The director of *Heaven Can Wait* took me into New York to see if I should start studying dramatics, because he had kind of a, you know, good thought about me. I said, 'Oh, come *on!*' ... because I didn't have acting in mind as a profession. Anyhow, I went into New York with him, to Maynard Morris in the MCA office, and he sent me over to the Alvin Theater on 52nd Street. There was about five hundred guys ahead of me — but damn if I didn't end up with a part. In *Mister Roberts!* Out of a plant I did ... you know ... I just changed my whole lifestyle.

"I was in the national company. I didn't play it in New York. We rehearsed it there, and then Hank Fonda joined us — which made our company number one — and I played in *Mister Roberts* on the road for *fifteen months*. Then we headed out here, producer Stanley Kramer sent me a telegram, I went on an interview, and I got into *High Noon*. That was my first show."

"Since you had been a farmhand, I suppose you were already a horseman, weren't you?"

"No, not really," Van Cleef said, "because it wasn't horses in Somerville. It was tractors and trucks on the farm. I didn't know beans about a horse until I got into film. As soon as I knew I was gonna be in *High Noon* when I came out here to California, then I got a guy that was in the stage play with me to go to a riding stable, and he taught me everything I knew, at that point in time. We went out *every bloody day* from sometime early in August until September 15, 1951, when I started to work. He had me doin' every kind of mount, dismount, run, walk, or any *other* darn thing on a horse, so that I could finally do the job properly in *High Noon*. And that guy that got me goin' on a horse, his name is Rance Howard, Ron and Clint Howard's father."

"Did you do a lot of the formal study associated with stagecraft while you were in the theater?" I asked. "Shakespeare? Dance?"

"I 'sharpened my tools' is the way I like to put it. I haven't studied Shakespeare because I don't like the Shakespearean style. But I *have* studied swords, I studied dance, voice, all the physical things I ever found I needed."

"Was this with the American Academy of — ?"

"No-o-o," Van Cleef interjected, "not with any academy. Just on my own. I went to the people that knew the stuff, and took private lessons."

"Do you not think formal study, training in the 'method' and so forth, are important to make a good actor?"

"I don't believe in what they call method acting. I don't know," he said, choosing his words carefully; "*I* don't believe in it. It could be good for some actors, but it's not good for me. As far as I'm concerned, method acting confuses audiences more than it tells them anything, and I think if you entertained them instead of confusing them, you'd get better results.

"Acting is a twisted up subject. I think to project yourself into another dimension, and then to make dimensions *within* the dimensions … I think that's an art form the same as music or painting or anything else. Or writing, in a sense, because even though you didn't write the original lines or ideas, to bring them to life is as much a form of art as the original thing. Anybody that can do the acting should be able to do the writing. In a lot of those European films, for example, I've done a lot of my own dialogue changes just to make it more compatible with my manner of speech, and my patterns, shall we say. I've never changed their ideas, just the way to say them or carry them out. Sometimes I even drop lines. Most actors like to add lines. They think the more they have, the better off they are. Bullshit! Sometimes I'd rather just use my eyes, use my face."

"More on that later," I forewarned. "But first, how did that long-standing stereotype as a villain get started? Was it doing the gunman in *High Noon* that locked you in place?"

"You're right. It started with *High Noon*, and that was it."

"You were one of Hollywood's biggest heavies all the time your three children were growing up. How did they handle that?"

"They handled it beautifully. *Beau*-tifully! No problem."

"Was Daddy always the hero when he got home?" I joked, a notion that amused him.

"I'd like to *think* so!" he laughed, then reflected soberly. "But … sometimes I wasn't even here for them. I'd be away on a job. I wasn't a heavy at home, but I wasn't a hero. I don't pretend to be a hero anyplace except perhaps on film. I believe in other dimensions. Now, my kids are kind of proud of what I did, so … everything turns out well."

"During those early years, was the chain of heavies completely unbroken?" I asked.

"Oh no. I did other things, but they were never recognized too much. Like, I did a guest-lead in 'The Medic,' that program Dick Boone starred in. I played a doctor in an episode called, I think, *Day Ten*, about the plague epidemic in L.A. back in the thirties."

"Frankly," I said, "while I've seen many of your films, what comes across in hindsight is not individual roles or movies so much—that is, prior to your move to Europe—as an overall impression of characters like the one you did in *Posse from Hell*. To me, he was the typical Van Cleef-style villain, a man so dangerous as to be almost infernally powered, a dreadfully bad human being. As the film opened, the outlaws strode into a saloon. Your character approached a milquetoast at the bar and without any warning proceeded to grab a whiskey bottle out of his hand. Unaccustomed to such rudeness, the man resisted. You matter-of-factly unsheathed a knife and cut his hand, a show of unadulterated spitefulness that totally disarmed him, and your icy stare propelled him clear across the room. Later, when the posse had ridden you down and gut-shot you, you begged them not to let you die there in the desert, claiming, 'Yew cain't leave me like this! Yer Christians, aintcha?!' It was the sorriest soul demanding mercy he, himself, would never have extended. He was the worst of bad eggs; in his malice, a step beyond your more common villains. How did you manage to project such heinous characters during those years, most of them seemingly motivated by an invincible evil?"

"Mmmmmmnh!" Van Cleef flinched. "I despised that film, for some reason. I don't know exactly why, but every time it comes on TV, I turn it off. But I've liked other ones. In fact, I haven't got one other one that I don't like.

"But the thing about playing a heavy is *don't* make yourself so completely invincible. That's what I've been trying to do with every damn picture since I knew what I was doing. I don't *want* to be so completely invincible, because I don't think that's *human*. You want to see a guy down on his knees cryin' for mercy, I did a picture called *The Bravados* — with Gregory Peck, Henry Silva, Stephen Boyd ... a lot of good ones in that one — where I was gonna get Peck, but he came around from the other direction, had his gun on me, there was nothing I could do. We went through that thing where he was showing me a picture of his wife in a watch, I swore I didn't know anything about it, he didn't believe me, and he plugged me right in the head. Shot me dead away."

(In *The Bravados*, Albert Salmi, Henry Silva, and Van Cleef were the central heavies; a white man, an Indian, and a half-breed. They were already arrested for capital crimes, had been convicted, faced the noose, broke jail, and circumstantial evidence pointed to them as the rapist-killers of Gregory Peck's wife. Peck tracked down the white man [Salmi] and half-breed [Van Cleef] and slew them in horrendously moving scenes. Not until the end of the picture, when Peck learned his wife's real murderers had been caught, was there any reason to credit the tortured cries of innocence from the two men just before they were killed. The bad taste left by *The Bravados'* executions — of guilty men, but for the wrong crime — was as strong as that left by those of innocent men in *The Ox-Bow Incident*.)

"I think I grew up a little with *The Bravados*," I conceded, "and for a piece of supportive acting, that may have been your finest. It was probably the first time I'd ever taken pity on a bad guy about to get blown away, something that had always seemed an entirely appropriate action beforehand."

"That's what I *look* for in film," Van Cleef declared. "Some place to have a bit of sympathy — *not* pity — but *sympathy*; so that the audience feels they're almost — *almost*, I say — as much on your side as they are on the leading man's. Once I learned what I was doin', which only took a picture or two, I tried to find some extra dimension to every character, a sympathetic area. Now, right or wrong, I've done that all these years. It gives you another thing to do. Sometimes you *don't* find 'em. But if you can, and use them, it helps; like patting a child on the head, instead of kickin' 'im in the ass. Never hurt a dog. I don't kick dogs. I don't pound women. I haven't slapped a woman yet on screen."

"You did that in *The Good, the Bad, and the Ugly*," I contradicted.

"That was done by a stunt man, not by me, because I refused to do it. The girl wanted to be slapped, actually slapped. I'm six-feet two, weight around one-ninety, two hundred, I'm fairly well put together. I've got a heavy hand, and I don't like to do things that could possibly hurt somebody, in any way."

"Playing the villain, is there anything special you consciously do to act malicious in a role?" I asked.

"Nnnn-no," he pondered, "I just believe what I'm doing, and have a respect for the other guy; and I've got to do it that way, it's as simple as that.

"And," he added, "I'm playin' three guys: myself, the character that I've read ... and that last guy in the balcony lookin' down at me. It's like bein' in three places at once. You're you, you're playin' the character —that makes two, right there—then, the guy that's watchin' it, so that you're able to actually *see* what you're doin' ... just like I'm lookin' into this microphone, right now. *There's* a point for anybody to learn from," he offered circumspectly.

"Since the invention of motion pictures," I said, "the Code of the West followed by so many of the traditional Western heroes has played some real part in the moral upbringing of three generations. As a villain, did you ever see yourself in a pedagogical function; that by the way you presented your character, you could turn young people off to that kind of person, and the wrong things he was doing?"

"That's ... a pretty good way to put it," Van Cleef said, mulling the notion over. "I think that's a very good way to put it," he concluded. "I have felt that the hero in a picture—if it's me, I want it to be a little bit of both ways—but if it's somebody else, say a Gene Autry or Jock Mahoney, Roy Rogers or whoever you want to say ... whatever I did as a heavy, I did as *heavy* as I *could*; then the other guy is that much stronger. And that's the way it should be, cause he's gotta win in the end. You *know* that. It's necessary to be as strong as possible in a fight scene or a gunfight or whatever, so the other guy comes out properly, even though I still tried at times to get a moment of sympathetic area doing the thing. I did the same thing as a hero, played it as strong as possible. I'm not in any way against violence if it's justified. I have played the bad guy, and *enjoyed* playing the bad guy ... but let the justification *tear—me—down*! Or, build me *up*, in case I'm the hero."

"In addition to *The Bravados*, was there anything else you did back then as a character heavy that you were particularly proud of?" I asked.

"I think that prior to the European move," he considered, "the things that I think about, more often than anything else that happened in major films back there, are the television jobs. There was a lot of good ones on there, even though it was made cheap and fast; and I enjoyed workin' with Bill Williams, and with Jock Mahoney ... uh ... darn! I can't think of all their names, so maybe I'd better not mention any more. But those things were really a great school for me. I learned from all of them, and I think I did some damn fine stuff."

"You spent half your career as a character actor before making your own films. I'm sure, like most actors, you had your lean times," I judged, "but would you do it all the same, if you could do it over?"

"Most definitely." Van Cleef's smooth, deep voice returned with hang tough resignation. "The only regrets I've got is the unhealthiness that can come out of idleness."

"What was your longest dry spell?"

"Oh, boy!" he groaned. "That's a good question. I don't know exactly what the length of the period was, but I think the worst one I had was just before the advent of the Italian Westerns."

"And how did they come about?" I questioned. "What led you to making pictures over there?"

"Money! *Mun*-nee!" he enunciated. "I'll admit it to you. I was broke! I couldn't pay my phone bill, and it wasn't all that big. They offered me more money than I ever made on any picture, and that's what started it. It was Sergio Leone who came over and said, I want you to do a thing. So I did it. It was the first one I did with Clint Eastwood, *For a Few Dollars More*. I left April the 12th, 1965; then exactly one year later I left on the second one, *The Good, the Bad, and the Ugly*. That went back-to-back with *The Big Gundown* where I starred on my own, instead of with Clint, and ... it's been goin' like that ever since. Goin' to the airport, gettin' on a plane, jumpin' one, two, six or twelve hours — maybe *twenty* hours — to one place or the other. I kept an apartment in Rome for a while at one point when those pictures were comin' so fast and furious. But I live here right now, basically, and I hope to stay that way."

"Are you still making films in Europe, though?"

"I'm making films wherever they're being *made*! Whether it's here, Israel, the Canaries, Spain, Italy, Yugoslavia — it doesn't make a damn bit of difference *where* they're made. It's an international business, everybody will eventually see what's done, and that's what the point is. It's not just makin' it in California. Bullshit! You gotta make 'em where they're bein' made. Unfortunately," he said with concern, "there's not enough being done *here*. We've got to somehow or another springboard the situation in this country. In the foreign countries, they get help. The government helps them. The government isn't helping *anything* here, in that regard. I think if they followed the examples of Italy or Spain, with tax rebates or whatever ... then there would be more money to make a picture and start another, and you can keep goin' from there. That's why the film industry in Europe is so much better than it is here."

"In a sense," I remarked, "Sergio Leone gave your career a second start, didn't he?"

"Well, you can't actually say it was a renewal in the business," he corrected. "It was just, thank God, I hung on and didn't go into something else, try to get a job diggin' ditches. This business, my friend, is ups and downs all the way for everybody. You don't know you're going to do anything until you're there with script in hand, in wardrobe, makeup, and you're in front of the camera and it's rollin'. Then you know you've got the job. And it's climbin' that ladder slowly, drop a couple of rungs and gain three. The best thing somebody can do is make the right kind of investments along the way when you *do* have it, so that you've got something to fall back on, and make sure you know how to do something else. I'm sure most actors do. I'd hate to see Charlie Bronson go back to the coal mines, because he's too damn good where he is. I don't want to go back to the farms, either. I wasn't that good a farmer. If I had to do something else — which I don't think I will — I'd go into another art form, or some other area within the business.

"But when Leone invited me over to Europe the first time, that *was* more money than I'd made on any show here. Everything's relative; there's a fourteen year difference, 1951 to 1965, but ... hell, my per diem, just the living expenses they gave me was as much as I made on my very first picture, the whole salary."

"That name 'Angel Eyes' in *The Good, the Bad, and the Ugly*; was that tailor-made specifically for you?" I asked.

"If it was in the script, I didn't see it," Van Cleef recalled, "and I'm usually pretty careful about giving scripts a close reading. I think Clint came out with it one day. It just kind of sprung out, and it was used ever since. I made no complaints about it. They've referred to me as that quite often in publicity since that time. I thought it was pretty good."

"Absolutely," I agreed. "How long did it take to make that film, by the way? Wasn't your typical Italian Western a rather fast piece of work?"

"Well, yes, in comparison to, say, *Cleopatra* or Brando's *Mutiny on the Bounty*, or some of those others which took many months, perhaps even over a year, the European jobs generally run anywhere from eight weeks to twelve. *The Good, the Bad, and the Ugly* only took thirteen weeks. But that's just *shooting* time," he stressed. "That's not preparation time; and all the post-production, which can take any length of time, six months or more to get all the little fine details of sound and editing in there they want. And Leone did all his own stuff in those days."

"Then they couldn't be called 'quickies'?"

"No. I've done pictures over here back in the fifties—my God! I'm not gonna tell you the titles of the darn things because I don't want to remember 'em. But in two or three weeks time we did *two* feature length pictures and parts of *three* different television shows. That was the fastest bunch of scramblin' that I've ever been on. In the old days, also, in the half-hour TV shows we'd do *three* a week, jumpin' from one script to another. All within one day I would have changed wardrobe maybe fourteen or fifteen times and bounced back and forth from one script to another many, many times within that period. With the hour shows, we'd get one done in five or six days. Sometimes they'll give a week and a half to that, now."

"What were your working conditions there, as far as language went. Did everyone speak English?"

"No. Not then. Everybody speaks English now, for the most part. For your somewhat better films, your major actors do speak English now, mostly; unless they're in there doin' somebody a favor and won't speak anything but their own tongue, which I think they're making a mistake there. And in some of your cheapies now, they won't. But in the old days—well, I say the old days, it was fourteen, fifteen years ago and before that—everybody would be speaking in their own tongue. Leone couldn't speak English to begin with. He speaks it very well now, but in the first picture he could hardly speak it at all, and we had an interpreter on both of the pictures I did for him. There was one scene in *For a Few Dollars More* that I was in where there were five languages spoken: Greek, Italian, German, Spanish, and a Cockney Englishman that I couldn't understand any better than I could understand the Greek! But I got along in it, because I knew what everybody was supposed to be saying in English by my script. So, when they'd stop speakin', then I would say something. Also, I began to pick up some of the Italian and Spanish which was prevalent over there."

"Did any of your fellow actors ever express or hint at any resentments towards you, as an American on a European set; as if to suggest you had taken the job away from a more deserving local?" I asked.

"No, I never felt it," Van Cleef said. "I think that the people in the know, they understand that as well as an art, it's an international business and a money game. Because it's international, you have people with different nationalities in damn near every film today. Even American producers will go over to Europe to get money to pre-sell a picture. As a consequence, to get this money, they may sometimes have to take actors and technicians from the countries they're negotiating with—or I'm sure in a lot of cases, they *want* to take them, because there's a lot of fine people abroad. So, if you're going to make a film anywhere, and you're going to want money from Italy, money from Spain, from Mexico, from Canada, then they will own a film for their particular areas, or however you negotiate it—there's no two alike—and you've got people from all over the world in one film.

"But we got along fine. No problem at all. You'd be surprised how many over there do speak English now, cause the actors have *had* to learn. It wasn't that way before. I'd usually pal around with somebody who commanded both English as well as the tongues of anybody there around me. The stunt man I had over there for quite some time spoke English very well, and both Spanish and Italian. My wife speaks a little bit of Spanish, too, and I speak enough Italian now to make myself understood.

"With the actors, it was no problem whatsoever. Somebody'd be around who could interpret if the goin' got a little bit thick. I've never had any problem in Europe or any place else I've been, except perhaps with producers; once in a while, a little bit of a tangle with a director. But if he could speak English well, and I could make my point clear enough and he agreed with it, then he'd do it my way. Otherwise I'd go ahead and do the best I could with it his way, unless I was totally against it. Then I just refused to do it, and that only happened once or twice. I don't like to infringe on another guy's territory unless it directly involves me, but there was one show over there, one of the early ones after I finished with Leone, and I directed myself all the way through the damn thing. I just couldn't take the director's directions. On occasion I even had to correct him on right and left, and where to set lights."

"On the other side of the coin," I asked, "were you ever treated with a certain deference, stemming from the fact that compared with your co-stars, your career has made you a bonafide veteran of the cowboy genre?"

"Well, sometimes I'd get the feeling they looked up at it, and sometimes I'd get the feeling they were wonderin' when I was goin' to fall off my *horse*! If ever. You know, you get that negative feeling every once in a while, even though there's no reason for it, that they're just *waiting* for you to make a mistake. Sounds like I walk around with a lot of confidence, I guess." Van Cleef laughed self-consciously. "But I haven't fallen flat yet. And I most often got the feeling that I was respected, and I got nothing *but* that. What went on behind my back, I'm not all that certain. But up in the foreground, I got all the respect that any one man can handle."

"Some of those pictures you made over there have been out long enough to make it to television. Do you ever watch yourself in them, or in *any* of the old reruns or the older pictures—excepting *Posse from Hell*, of course?"

"*Liberty Valance* was on just the other night here. The only reason I didn't see it again is I've seen it so many times already. I'll watch a picture if I liked *it*, on an overall basis—which is what I aim at. I don't aim at pointin' *myself* up. I aim at a good picture overall, which I think *Liberty Valance* was. When it comes to film work—at least the ones that I'm in — whether I'm playin' the heavy or the lead, I don't give a damn. I just want the picture to be direct, I want the people to understand it, and I want 'em to go home satisfied."

"I get the impression from a fairly crowded list of pictures covering the last ten years," I said, "that you belong among those performers who like to call themselves 'working actors.' That is, sometimes you will accept an assignment for the sake of staying in the game, keeping the creative juices flowing."

"Well, yeah, but I don't do it at the risk of dropping quality," Van Cleef retorted. "That's why I stick to motion pictures. If I do end up doing television, it would be because the script is damn good and there is room for good characterization in the thing for as long as the program will go. I pick and choose. I don't work for the sake of working. I don't *believe* in that. I've got *other* things I do to keep my juices flowing — and I'm *not* talkin' about beer and alcohol! My home takes a lot of creativity. I've got juices flowin' all *over* the place here, between the painting and wood-working and the rest. I paint. I write scripts and songs. I sing and play music. My wife Barbara is very musical. She's a concert pianist. She can solo, accompany; even play clubs, because she not only does the classical, but she can go into darn near any area of music on the piano. I've picked up on music along the way in my career, but I concentrated on it pretty hard in school, too; played trombone and sang. As a little child I played piano. Now I just fool around with a guitar to aid me in creating songs. I sketch a lot. I paint in oils and acrylics; landscapes, primarily seascapes ... and figure. Female form." He owned cheerily, "I'm still healthy."

"Obviously you have plenty to keep you occupied within the confines of your home," I said. "But when you do venture out, can you move about freely in public, here or abroad? Your rather unique features, after all, have been seen far and wide, and had impact over a long career both as the rugged villain and sturdy hero."

"I don't like to get out too much," he said. "I like going out to supper, or something like that; but I don't like to get out into crowds, like going to Disneyland or Knott's Berry Farm, or such places. On a street in Rome, I don't seem to worry about it too much. The only thing that bothers me over there is the paparazzi. *They* bug the *hell* out of me."

"Did your presence in a restaurant or bar ever spark a hostile reaction from somebody out to prove his manhood?" I asked.

"Ho, ho, ho-o-o-o! You better *know* it! It's happened more here than in Europe, but it *has* happened there. Not in Italy. Only once in Spain, once in the Canaries; that was it. The rest of it's been in California, but not really all that much, and more often in bars than restaurants."

"How do you handle somebody who's forcing that screen machismo on the real you, in the middle of a drink or dinner?" I inquired.

"Try to talk out of it," he said. "If you can't talk out of it — then you back it up."

"You mean, quietly leave?"

Van Cleef's voice levelled out. "Bill, I've never *started* a brawl. You *try* to quietly leave, but if it doesn't happen, then ... you know what you've gotta do."

"You've had to do it."

"Yes," he declared. "Yes. That doesn't mean that I'm *proud* of it. But I've had to do it."

I backtracked. "You said before that you wanted your films to be direct, and you wanted people to understand them, and to go home satisfied."

"Yeah, I want 'em to go home satisfied that they've seen somebody do the best job they can. That's not just me. That's anybody I'm in the picture with. And I want 'em to go home entertained. In other words, I don't like disappointments, you know, walkin' out of the theater that way. I don't go back quite as soon."

"But surely you recognize there are other kinds of satisfaction outside of happy endings," I argued. "Wouldn't you be willing to go out on a limb in a picture, do something a little bit elliptical, something that isn't straightline adventure, with all the traditional factors involved?"

"Well, yeah, certainly," Van Cleef replied. "Naturally, it would depend on the script. There again, I'm after good material. Maybe I said it in a way that could be misunderstood, but when I say 'direct,' I mean simple and to the point, without *too* many complications within a character, so that you don't know where the character is ... or where he 'comes from,' I think is the modern way of saying it. There's *gotta* be a *solution* to a thing. I've seen too many free-form type endings where there's absolutely *no* solution to it at *all*! There was one on television here the other night about a car theft ring. It had some pretty fair chases in it and all that sort of thing, but after all the devastation, the guy gets away scot free at the end. The *bad* guy got *away* with it and rode out of the picture with his girl or something ... or at least with the car. Maybe the car represented his girl, I don't know. We find things like that hidden in some of these stories, too."

"In your opinion, then, justice must prevail?" I asked.

"Not necessarily 'justice'," he said, putting a finer point on it. "I think the *truth* should. If a thief gets away with it, let him not be trafficking in the wrong stuff. Let's not show the *rapist* or *murderer* getting away with it — unless it's some kind of documentary you're filming — but neither one of those. Otherwise, *I* don't want to be involved."

"It seems your presence on film has provoked strong reactions from the critics," I posed. "On the positive side, several have expressed admiration for you as an actor; but by and large, few have been able to find kind words for the type of pictures you've done since striking out on your own. The general tone of the reviews — even when favorable to you, personally — is scornful of what you described as your 'outdoor adventures'."

"I don't think the critics know what the hell they're talking about sometimes," Van Cleef shot back. "I don't see anything wrong with a good honest approach in a film, and a good deal of feeling that somebody's put into it. I don't see anything wrong with that at all. No, I don't believe in the critics. Usually when they get negative, they bring in more people to the show than they turn away."

"The lack of critical acclaim doesn't bother you?"

"I don't think there *was* any lack of critical acclaim, on the Leone pictures. Some of the others," he warranted, "I can understand ... but I don't agree with! I don't believe in an awful lot of what the critics do. This local newspaper we've got here in Los Angeles knocked the *hell* out of me on pictures that I think were damned *good*. *El Condor*, for instance, where I played kind of a humorous heavy. They really wanted to knock *that* one out of the *box*! But nevertheless, it came out, and people have enjoyed it."

"One reason for the opprobrium your pictures have drawn, obviously, is the prevalent violence in their content," I stated, "something we're finding universally condemned lately in movies and television. The theory goes, of course, that imitations of — that buzz word — violence, by actors, would leak out into the surrounding society in the form of real criminal acts."

"Yeah, I understand you," Van Cleef responded wearily.

"Suppose, hypothetically, you were hauled before the P.T.A. or some other anti-violence-in-media group, and in some kangaroo court scenario, you were prosecuted for your work in films. What would be your defense? Would you just tell them to frig off?"

"Besides sayin' *that*," he laughed, "I would just say basically, '*I* am an *actor*; and I will do goddamn near *anything*, as long as it doesn't go against my grain. And that would include belting women, kicking dogs, or hurting children. I won't do things of that nature'."

"Have you really rejected scripts on that principle?" I pressed. "Scripts that were passed on to, and done by someone else?"

"True. Very true," Van Cleef affirmed. "But basically I would say I am an actor, that I enjoy what I'm doing and want to continue doing it, I want the public to enjoy it as much as I do, and that I'll never quit, until I'm dead. The things I do in a movie, I try to justify. If it's not in the script, I can't justify it; but if it's *in* the script, I *will*. What the *real* bad guys are doing is something entirely different. What *they're* doing is out on the *street*. My *movies'll* play on the street, but *I'm* not doing anything on the street. I'm in there to do a job; just like the P.T.A., or whoever, is out to do their job ... when they're *doin'* it, instead of horsin' around!

"I don't think it should be shown that the rapist, or murderer, or something like that gets away with it," he said. "That's when it begins to get a little sticky, because some goddarn nut — who's probably nuts *already* — will probably go out and *try* some dumb thing. That's what they say about too much violence on screen, which I don't agree with, because if they showed violence as *realistically* as it can be, then that would be a *deterrent*. But they don't. They make it look like fun and games, and you don't see the gore and blood. Then is when you're gonna have trouble, because it doesn't look like anybody gets hurt when they get punched in the mouth. *Try* it sometimes! Jesus Christ.

"I think the more gory violence is made, the more realistic, the *better* it is. And that way, I do *not* think it is anything that's gonna entice anybody — unless they're *already* nuts! That doesn't necessarily agree with a lot of psychiatrists and psychologists, but it's my personal opinion. Show *war* as it is. Nobody'll want to go to war. They don't want to go to war *now*, because they've *seen* it."

"As you certainly have," I said. "I understand your naval service in World War II took you to the Caribbean on a submarine chaser; then through the Mediterranean, Black and China seas on a mine sweeper. In effect, as a very young man you had seen the world, but a world half destroyed by war. What was the sensation of going back to many of these places years later, not as a sailor, but as a film star, and seeing them in peace and prosperity?"

"Well, it's *always* a thrill to see a place when it's not at war," Van Cleef stated the obvious. "When we went over to Israel to make a couple of pictures, I had my wife with me. And she wanted to go to Jerusalem *so* bad. But a journalist I was having an interview with said, *'Don't go to Jerusalem!'* Because they weren't printing half of what the actual damage and killing was, at that particular point. That was a few years ago when all holy hell was breakin' loose there. They would only print a portion of it. They wouldn't tell of all the innocent bystanders that got it, shot or stoned or blasted with a bomb. So wherever there's any turmoil in this world in any shape or form, and I'm aware of it, I avoid it. I won't take my wife into it, and I won't go anywhere without her."

"She accompanies you on location?"

"She goes with me *everywhere*. Most generally, we're together on all occasions. We made a pact when we first got married, back in 1976, that if she goes on a concert tour, I go with her. If I'm on a picture, she goes with me, and that's the way it's been. It's a mutual agreement. I don't push her into anything. I don't have to. She's more than willing to please me, just like I am willing to please her.

"And we respect each other's need to be alone once in a while, too. That counts for a lot. She likes to go walk on the beach, wherever we are; as she did in Israel, and up and down our own coasts here," Van Cleef said. A hard edge in his voice had disappeared, possibly as the mental pictures of actual, headline-making villains were replaced by one more tender. "I let her go wanderin' off," he said. "So, she's off on her own, just like I'm alone with my own thoughts. She can't see me ... but I've got my eye on her, my safety eye. Nothing's going to happen to her."

Footprints in the sand, a brush on canvas, keyboard duets, hearth and home. Such idyllic pastimes are not the wages of cinematic sin. Fortunately, real life has been kinder to Lee Van Cleef. Add one more reward so contrary to the deserts of most of his screen characters, one he would agree has been the best.

He got the girl. [October 1979.]

III

The Rednecks

"Now, I appeal to every human mind, imbued with the commonest of common sense, and the commonest of common humanity ... and ask, with these revolting evidences of the state of society which exists in and about the slave districts of America ... Will they say of any tale of cruelty and horror, however aggravated in degree, that it is improbable, when they can turn to the public prints, and, running, read such signs as these, laid before them by the men who rule the slaves: in their own acts and under their own hands?

"Do we not know that the worst deformity and ugliness of slavery are at once the cause and effect of the reckless license taken by these free-born outlaws? ... [T]hat the man who has been born and bred among its wrongs ... whenever his wrath is kindled up, will be a brutal savage? ... [T]hat as he is a coward in his domestic life, stalking among his shrinking men and women slaves armed with his heavy whip, so he will be a coward out of doors, and carrying cowards' weapons in his breast, will shoot men down and stab them when he quarrels? And ... should we not know that they who among their equals stab and pistol in the legislative halls, and in the counting-house, and on the marketplace, and in all the elsewhere peaceful pursuits of life, must be to their dependants ... so many merciless and unrelenting tyrants?

"What! shall we declaim against the ignorant peasantry of Ireland, and mince the matter when these American taskmasters are in question? ... Shall we whimper over legends of the tortures practiced by the Pagan Indians, and smile upon the cruelties of Christian men!"

So wrote Charles Dickens in *American Notes* recorded on his first visit to this country. He arrived in 1842 already bearing a hate for the practice of slave-holding. Abolitionist literature, widely circulated in England, had stoked his revulsion for the degrading institution, tales of which had been so ghastly, Dickens must have assumed they were smuggled from remote hellholes at great risk. His tour took him no farther south than Richmond, Virginia, but—while the slave conditions he witnessed firsthand were relatively mild—newspapers he scanned throughout his travels openly confirmed his worst expectations. Through advertisements masters inquired after runaways, brazenly cataloguing "identifying marks" from which one could easily deduce the tortures fugitives had already suffered. Dickens was even more appalled by the abundance of news items relating, as a matter of course, the violence committed by free whites not only against blacks, but against each other in the Southern states.

From Dickens' era to the present, the Southern white's reputation of being violence-prone, bigoted and uncivil is a deserved one in many cases. Atrocities of boastful hooligans acting in the name of white supremacy, "decency," "tradition," or God Himself are a permanent blemish on Southern history. Consequently in Hollywood's contributions to the cause of civil rights, the redneck has become a staple heavy for the movies; and because of filmed preachments against racism and backwardness, the South is generally perceived as the national stronghold of intolerance, dwarfed intellect, and brutality.

Such an unflattering depiction mirrors truth — with considerable exaggeration, it should be noted. Dramatic content, after all, requires a reality heightened and amplified over any viewer's personal humdrum version. But frequently the redneck villain has been so overstated as to stretch far beyond the limits of a reasonably credible human character. A lumbering semiliterate voicing an affected moonlight-and-magnolias accent has detracted from the serious motives of many an otherwise worthy film or teledrama. To avoid the distractions of an imprecise Southern characterization, Hollywood has three solutions. One is to hire an actor facile in the handling of quaint dialects. Another is the *Gone with the Wind* ploy — that is, to ignore the matter completely, going so far as to cast British performers in most major roles. The third solution is: Go to the source. Hire an actor born and reared among the habits and speech of the South.

Solution Three has yielded very impressive results and, contrary to what the South's image makers would have led us to believe, it never involved some cinéma vérité arrangement where a genuine rube mouthed his lines and took payment in beer and shotgun shells. At least, this is hardly the case with Bo Hopkins, Luke Askew and Bill McKinney, three skillful and highly experienced actors. As native Southerners they have portrayed extra-effective redneck heavies, and excelled as good ol' boys, rustics, and other assorted rough-cuts, meanwhile injecting a realism that only actors of their background could have provided. The advantage of their birth has freed them from overwhelming efforts to concoct bizarre accents and mannerisms, and allowed them to concentrate on the personality of whatever role was at hand.

When Hopkins, Askew and McKinney are villainous on film, their villainy can be on that same horrific scale that outraged Dickens. But behind the vile façade one senses a more universal figure. We see, blinkingly, that we can slap no regional, racial, nor ethnic label onto their crimes; that the motives of fear, hate and pride are not the products of a Southern monopoly. And when in the shoes of a character these three show an ounce of loyalty or true courage, hold back a punch, break out with a grin that splits faces all around, or open a fist to shake another's hand; then they dignify the Southern stereotype, and reveal him to be no higher nor lower a creature than the rest of humanity.

A baby-faced, flaxen-haired kid rolled up his big blue eyes and defiantly moaned to his killers, "How'dya like to kiss my sister's black cat's ass?" It set the tone for the rest of *The Wild Bunch* in which vulgar, violent men traded shots and gutter insults with little pause. The dying lad's shock value stemmed not only from his foul tongue, but as well from a handiness with a shotgun earlier in the movie's initial gunbattle. Nor did his fresh features seem to belong on one who had sunk so low in so few years; but in his portrayer's film debut, twenty-four-year-old Bo Hopkins put across with ease the part of a raw youth.

Four years later Hopkins could still trade on youngish looks while playing gang leader of the Pharaohs in *American Graffiti*—but no longer. Ten years after *The Wild Bunch*, his eyes deeper set, hair prematurely grizzling and slightly coarser, and a face lined with accrued cunning, the more seasoned actor has finished a long apprenticeship playing hot-tempered hillbilly boys, swaggering rubes, and drawling badasses, including a few bumpkin caricatures for television that—not by his own choice—bordered on the ludicrous.

Outgrowing the redneck stereotype, Hopkins has emerged as one of Hollywood's newest leading men, much in demand for television projects, and with *A Small Town in Texas* and *Tentacles* to his credit as starring vehicles. Still, there is a quality from Hopkins' earlier roles that has followed him up the ladder, and will likely remain; a capacity for playing it cool and tough. Primarily a sympathetic heavy, he has made a roguish prop of the dangling cigarette, living up to the best traditions of Bogart and Belmondo. In his most threatening guises, wild-eyed and smiling, ever smiling—as with his gunslinging cowhand of *Culpepper Cattle Company*, or his borderline-psycho weapons expert in *The Killer Elite*—there has always been a manic air about him. The moral taint is still evident, often laughably, in his semiregular stint on *The Rockford Files* as John Cooper, possessor of a fine legal mind and just the right amount of duplicity to have gotten himself disbarred. Then again, as "Tex," the American "narc" and Billy Hayes's unsympathizing compatriot in *Midnight Express*, he was not so funny. But even from the ruffian's standpoint Hopkins has presented characters with a great sensitivity. In *The Man Who Loved Cat Dancing* an aloof Englishwoman was kidnapped by trainrobbers, and became variously an object of lust and scorn to her low-bred captors. In the bandit played by Hopkins, however, an infatuation with the proper lady blossomed; and his gallantry on her behalf, even as he lay dying, made for a touching portrayal. Seen more recently as a mob flunkey in television's *Aspen* miniseries, he committed a sex-murder and framed an innocent friend. In the closing scene he confessed all, with impunity, to the friend and friend's lawyer. Hopkins' guilt-haunted, tearful dissolve and skulking exit—on a level of acting above and beyond the small screen's usual call—unerringly personified a man wearing the mark of Cain.

A working class upbringing in his native South Carolina provided plenty of grist for playing redneck and rustic heavies, but low odds that Bo Hopkins would ever deliver them to stage or screen. Embarking on an acting career, beginning with the local community playhouse, Hopkins packed a deeply troubled background along. The death of his father emotionally shattered him at age nine, and left scars. Hopkins also had a short-lived, teenage have-to marriage and a problematic Army hitch behind him, no high school diploma, and a tendency to raise hell under-the-influence; but he advanced to regional theater in Kentucky, and eventually found himself in New York studying under Stella Adler. Sophisticated young men and women surrounded him there, lofty schooling and affluence marking their conversations, attitudes and apparel. Hopkins quickly figured his success as an actor depended on closing scholastic and cultural gaps between himself and his peers. Although a drop-out, he had formerly been an apt pupil. On his own he devised a refresher course of study, and readjusted intellectually for the literate profession he had entered. Perhaps more importantly, he stopped playing Lone Ranger against emotional hang-ups, sought professional help, and developed self-discipline over his bent for liquor and brawling.

Ultimately Hopkins appeared Off-Broadway, performed live theater when he first moved to the West Coast, and still considers the stage a practical option. When we spoke, he had just returned from doing *Picnic* in Greeneville, S.C., his first hometown engagement in a decade. He credited his experience in theater as the best place for any actor to start, a place to broaden one's range of characters in a quick succession of plays. "And then, you get a lot of training you don't even realize," he told me. "A lot of self-confidence, a lot of ability to motivate yourself. You learn a lot of will power, because you know you can't stay out late drinkin' and then still perform." Stage training, however, was not entirely adequate for Hollywood cameras. "Unfortunately, plays are different from movies or television," he said, "because you have to hit a mark, you've got your cue light, and there's a million things you don't know about. I think that drama schools should also teach camera techniques to actors. You've been taught to believe in what you're doin' and sayin', then you get in a movie, and it's scary where you're supposed to be riding a horse and they put you up on a *ladder*! You have to get used to those things."

Hopkins was candid about his sheepskin deficiency, a fact to which he had finally reconciled himself, although he described a self-consciousness he had during his early days in New York as a "fear of stupidity." Able to view it now with some perspective, he reflected, "I hope maybe one day I might go back and finish—but I *know* now that I *can survive*; because most of the people I've met, even with their educations—a lot of them in this business are well educated—no matter how many books you read, that doesn't *stop* you from being stupid! I don't have a 'fear of stupidity' now that I've met a lot of producers in this business...," he snickered, leaving the sentence open-ended.

Hopkins continued, "Because of the fact that I quit school, and I went out into the world before I was supposed to, I had to try to catch up. And I felt insecure around people that had gone on, because even all my friends back home went on to college. But I found that I can do things on stage—playing senators, presidents, captains in the army, a private, whatever—I can do *all* those things. They have only one thing, one way to go; but I enjoy acting because I can play all the people that I know— every different kind of job—and still get paid for it, too. In other words, I can do something as good as they can, but I didn't have the education ... and that's my own fault. I'm not blaming anybody for that."

Bo Hopkins' Southern origin would be no mystery were he caught away from the cameras. He speaks, as himself, not in a hick Deep South drawl, but in the soft, fluid Coastal Southern dialect. Even if he is on camera, the chances are good he is playing a Westerner (*Monte Walsh, Culpepper Cattle Company, Posse*) or an indigenous or transplanted Southerner (*The Getaway, The Killer Elite, The Moonshine War, White Lightning*). He acknowledged the typecast, but only as a means to getting himself established, not as a permanent condition. "Jack Nicholson played in twenty-five motorcycle and horror movies before *he* got a break and got out of that mold," he reminded me. "I say that an actor, if he can act, it doesn't matter *what* kind of accent he has. Akim Tamiroff to me was one of the best actors I loved to watch. He was an old character actor and had, you know, a *Russian* accent, but you never paid any attention to that because of his *acting*. In other words, I'm tryin' to say that because I've got a Southern accent doesn't mean that I'm *like* any of those people I play, because I'm *different*."

"What about playing the heavy so often?" I asked him. "Any misgivings?"

"I think that some actor that starts out playin' these so-called *nice* guys that always get the girl or whatever ... people remember the *characters* that are surrounding him; and if he's surrounded by good characters, that makes *him* look better. When you come out of a movie, who do *you* remember? *I* would remember the *bad* guy. Those kinds of characters you can get into and have fun with, playing them. But," he said, his enthusiasm flagging, "I'm going to have to get into a whole new ball game. That's what acting's about, you know. I don't want to keep doin' the same thing, because ... hell, there's no *challenge* after a while. I won't *play* psychos any more because of that reason, unless it's an extra good script."

"What about the redneck characters?" I asked. "Some of them, like the whiskey runner in *White Lightning* and the sheriff of *A Small Town in Texas*, were pretty straightforward. But once on *Gunsmoke* long ago you played Festus' cousin, and your costume and makeup—a tattered peaked hat, bib overalls with one unhooked gallus, and blacked-out teeth—were straight out of Dogpatch."

"That's changed for me, because I won't take parts like that anymore." Hopkins bristled at being reminded of that cretinous ridge-runner and, no doubt, other characters of the same ilk. "I don't think it's *right!*" he protested. "I always said that on television there should be some Southern doctors, because a lot of friends of mine in my home town are doctors now. People from the South go to Yale and Harvard, you know. People out here are still fightin' the damn Civil War, and that's bullshit!"

"Just as movies and television have given a rather unbalanced view of the South, people could easily get a distorted picture of Bo Hopkins. Do you have an image problem from being a recurrent heavy?" I asked.

"Sometimes people think that I walk down the street at night with a stiletto hangin' out," he chuckled, "but, no. The thing about that is, if you're doin' your job the way you're supposed to be doin', that's the way it's supposed to come out. Most people, when the movie's over, remember the bad guys and tend to forget that the bad guy that's portrayed on the screen in *real* life—Vincent Price is a connoisseur of cooking ... Jack Elam kept books... I could go on—but actors are no different from other people. They go to the bathroom, they have fears. There's a lot of baloney about Hollywood, fast livin', orgies, fancy cars. I have a Mercedes, bought it last year—but I *worked* for it and saved my money just like anybody *else* that buys a car. The only difference between actors and other people is that they are in the public eye."

Under that public eye Hopkins seems to have found wide acceptance. "I'd just about got through with *A Small Town in Texas*," he said, "and some people down there are very nice. I was comin' out of the theater one night with Susan George, and this cop came up and said, 'Where ya parked?' Suddenly I got to thinkin' (you get paranoid) 'Uh-oh, I left a beer in the car,' and I said, 'Out back.' And he said, 'Oh, well, I'll just walk on out with ya,' and I said, 'Well, what's the problem?' And he said, 'I just wanted to make sure nobody bothered you.' But I appreciate the fact that people take time out to go see my work, and if it wasn't for them, I probably wouldn't be workin'. I think that's the point of acting. It's carryin' the theme and makin' it as honest and believable as you can, and doin' the best job you can. I enjoy feedback especially from kids. Kids take their time, act like they truly appreciate your signing somethin' for 'em. They'll talk to you. Grownups are *worse* than kids. When I was with

Burt Reynolds doin' *White Lightning* one time, there was two hundred adults *chargin'* us, tryin' to get at *him*. Now *that* was *scary!*"

"You had a pretty shaky start as an actor," I observed. "Have you finally reached a point where you feel secure? Not just financially, but in matters of personal esteem?"

"Oh, yeah. Yeah, I won't let the business *get* to me anymore. *I* want to get to the *business*. I'm willing to act with anyone who wants to act. I'm not scared to go out onto a stage with *Olivier* now." It was bold talk from one with his initial credentials.

"That's pretty stiff competition," I said.

"Competition isn't the point," Hopkins countered. "You're out there to work together, and one person don't make a show."

"Assuming even greater success is in store for you, do you think the adjustments you make for it will be as great as when you first began?"

"I don't think it will change me. I might have to get into my income tax a little more. But I don't worry now about the scariness of the business like I did six or seven years ago," he repeated. "I haven't reached my potential. I am nowhere near where I want to be as an actor, but I have proved that I can do what I *want* to do. And I don't let acting run my life. I'll run my *own* life. If I'm unhappy at acting—I don't think that'll happen, but if that were the case—I'm not as scared now that I couldn't *do* anything else. I could go around and tour colleges now and talk about it, or teach it, or participate in plays or, you know ... there's a *lot* of things I could do now; whereas when you first start out as an actor, you're so damned insecure that you suck your *thumb*. Like anyone else starting out when he graduates from college, he don't go right into the big executive room unless his dad owns the buildin'. So it's like anything else. You have your insecurities.

"But there comes a basic time when acting's not that most important thing in my life," Hopkins declared. "*I* am. And if I can't be happy in my work, then I'll find something else. You know, it's nice to read about yourself, but you've also got to live with yourself; and if it seems all phony to you and you can't separate the reality from the fiction part of it, then I think it'd be time to get out." [May 1976.]

After an Air Force hitch and undegreed terms at Mercer University and the University of Georgia, Luke Askew gravitated to New York City because "it just seemed like a good place to be." For thirteen years he moved furniture, washed dishes, held the usual assortment of jobs aspiring actors do without having any serious intentions himself of adopting the trade; but Macon, Georgia's native son was "more or less discovered," and hired to play redneck "Dolph Higginson" for the film *Hurry Sundown*. Six weeks after *Sundown*'s completion he joined the cast of *Cool Hand Luke* as "Boss Paul."

Since these initial acting ventures, for which Askew complacently owns to no formal preparatory training, he has compiled an impressive rogues' gallery. A mellow sort of fellow is scarce among his numerous screen and television characters. Most are lethal, some are sympathetic, many are not. There are elite soldiers: a court-martialled rapist dredged from the stockade into *The Devil's Brigade*, and Provo, a gung-ho country boy in *The Green Berets*. There are Westerners: one of the Younger brothers in *The Great Northfield, Minnesota Raid*, a hired gun with the *Culpepper Cattle Company*, a crack shot deputy in *Posse*, and in *Pat Garrett & Billy the Kid* a pal of the latter. And there are Southerners: a stone-hearted guard in *Cool Hand Luke*, a big-time moonshiner and Tennessee sheriff Buford Pusser's nemesis in *Walking Tall II*, and a trigger-man in the civil rights workers' murders of television's *Attack on Terror: The FBI vs. the KKK*. For such a dangerous, unsavory run of parts—both deplorable and sympathetic—the term "shitkicker" strongly suggests itself. Notwithstanding Luke Askew's skillful impersonations and bona fide Dixie roots, however, he hardly sounded like the type, as I remarked to him during our phone conversation. "Not at all," he responded in his characteristic husky drone. "Not in the least. Neither are the other people that you see." Regarding "Higginson," his debut role, he groaned, "I couldn't stand him. He was a despicable person."

"Was it a realistic role?" I asked.

"Oh yeah," he said. "I was born and raised with those people. There were people like that around everywhere." Despite his reprehension for the character, and the one that followed in *Cool Hand Luke*, I noted how each seemed to have a certain authenticity, but a conspicuous lack of overstatement. "Right," he concurred. "Up till that time, that particular type of Southern heavy was usually played by somebody who just couldn't get it across. Too much accent. Too much good ol' boy grabassing which really doesn't go on that much."

An honest concern for realism stood out as Askew discussed his work. Of all his films he had been most satisfied with *Culpepper Cattle Company* for its play dirty, shoot first for survival depiction. "I think it's one of the few times or pictures," he said, "that Western gunmen were ever represented in the way they probably really were."

"Why do you think your career has practically confined you to the action genre," I asked, "chiefly in Westerns—*Culpepper*, *Will Penny*, *The Magnificent Seven Ride*, *Posse*, others—and usually as some shade of heavy?"

"I think it depends a lot on how you got started," Askew replied. "I started off as a bad guy, and I've been one for quite some time; good/bad guy, totally bad guy, whatever. And the people who produce or direct Westerns have pretty set ideas about what Western people look like."

"You've been recast in that role because you have the look?"

"Wel-l-ll ... no. You have to be good. It's not just the look or an accent. You've gotta be *good*. You've gotta be able to get the *feeling* across. People out there looking have to believe that you *would* shoot 'em down."

At this, Askew is good. A slack-jawed, trim six-footer, his appearance lends itself easily to the image of a man unshaken by danger, reckless of its outcome. His saucer eyes look ready-made for laying dollars over the lids.

A gunslinger's easy slouch and icy scowl — Askew has displayed them frequently, but off chances have also permitted him to exercise a dry, ironic style of comic delivery. One of his most commendable rusks of witticism befell as he played the inscrutable hitchhiker in 1969's *Easy Rider*. It was an off-beat character, neither physically menacing nor warmly chummy. As if perched on a separate mental plane from the rest, he rebuffed the garrulous Billy (played by director Dennis Hopper) with oblique retorts. The hitchhiker, Billy and Wyatt sat smoking marijuana around their campfire, and a ponderous question arose: Did you ever want to be anyone else? The hitchhiker calmly offered, "I thought I'd try Porky Pig." There had to be a story behind that line, certainly one of the movies' hippest quips, so I asked him for it.

"I haven't got the *slightest* idea what I meant by that!" Askew laughed. "It just popped into my head and I *said* it. That was all ad-lib. We didn't have anything written for that scene. We didn't know what we were going to do until the time that it was done."

"But if the line didn't fit into the context, as it did, it would have found its way to the cutting room floor," I argued, clinging to a belief in the remark's having some kind of significance.

"Well, I don't know about that. Dennis is good at spotting that kind of thing, but for the most part you can't rely on anything winding up on the cutting room floor because it's *bad*. Some of the *best* stuff in a picture winds up on the floor. They want a film ninety minutes, you see? If they do a two-hour movie, you can only show it twice a day. They do a ninety-minute movie, you can show it *three* times a day."

As the "Porky Pig" line had come so automatically to Askew, apparently playing the heavy had been only slightly more demanding. No deep introspection for him, no packet of self-justifications to help him build a character. He merely pointed to the real world as a source of models, saying, "You *have* to know that there are people like the people I play, because you *see* them. They're around. You run into them. They always *have* been around, and they always *will* be."

"It doesn't sound like your approach to acting is all that formal," I posed.

"Not at all, unh-unh. A script is the kind of thing you can read through in one night, and it's just a question of discovering what kind of attitude you think the guy ought to have. You get it and hold on to it, and from then on, everything comes out right."

"In your experience as an actor, is there such a thing as a 'success formula'?" I asked. "A way of knowing whether to take a small role in a big picture, or risk taking a big role in a small production?"

"I'd much rather do, if I had my choice, a big part in a small picture, because it might *get* you somewhere. You never know *what* might happen behind something like that. *Easy Rider* was a 'small' picture. There's not that much of a risk to it. The truth of the matter is, if you're good, and you put your time in productively—you're gonna do fine."

"As long as you try, and have the talent?"

"Well ... whatever 'talent' *is*. It's hard to *say*. It doesn't necessarily have to be good acting. The main thing is to have some kind of appeal. I just think that, uh ... most interviewers' questions fit into one category or the other of 'How do you feel creatively...?' So on and so forth. The thing about it is, an actor has, to some extent, to *submerge* those things, *realizing* that he's working with a *business*; and be *patient*, and just do his work, and get better and move up ... and *get* there."

"Have you gotten there?"

"Well," Askew said, "the way this business works today, it's what you call 'incipient.' I mean, it could be tomorrow. It could be any day. It has to be a good part that attracts attention in a winning movie."

Luke Askew's career taught him early to view film acting with a cold eye. As with *Easy Rider*, his part constituted a wry joke—"Provo's Privy," in very grim taste—for 1968's *The Green Berets*. The movie's pro-Vietnam stance totally violated his feelings about the war—and yet, he took the job. "Would you ever take part again in something you disagreed with so strongly?" I asked.

"It would depend on what condition I was in. I wasn't that well established at the time of *The Green Berets*. It got me up from feature class to co-star class, paid me about three times as much as I was accustomed to making, so on that basis, I did it. I would have been a fool not to."

"You're content to have it on your résumé, then?"

"Yeah!" he asserted. "It was a viable, valid piece of work. I did a good job, no matter how I feel about the picture as a whole. People in the business view it *completely* unsentimentally. See, they don't give a damn about one side of the war or the other. All they care about is did the picture make money, and how you looked in it."

Queried about his most recent activities, Askew mentioned a few television assignments, then faded. "Let's see," he pondered. "Most of the pictures I've done are already out, and I can't even remember what they are, right offhand. I forget most of the stuff as soon as I've done it because I'm on something else by then. By the time *you* see a picture, I probably did it almost a year ago."

"This is not meant as criticism," I ventured, "but unfortunately, your television guest credits hardly seem to loom as large as even your more incidental ones in film."

"That's right," he agreed. "But television is like bread and butter. You do guest shots on television, you get big billing, and you get good money. I suppose they just put you in there for the prestige. I'm not sure what it's all about, but since everybody gets pretty much the same treatment, you don't feel badly about it at all. You just take the money and walk."

"Would you do a series?"

"I don't know. One of the main reasons I'd hate to do it would be having to live in L.A. for that length of time. I don't live in LA.," he explained. "I live a sort of country gentleman existence on my avocado ranch about a hundred miles away. When there's something to do for television, my agent gives me a call, I come in, check it out, and I'm usually gone from home a week."

"What do you have against Los Angeles?"

"L.A. is one of the most *miserable* places in the world to live! It's ugly, dull and smoggy. *Smog!*" he rasped. "It's *loaded* with smog! A *very* unhealthy place to live!"

"Discounting the boost a TV series could give you, and until that appealing part in a winning picture comes along, this leaves you in co-star status or, less often now, as a character actor. Monetarily, has it been worth your while so far?"

"Well, things have happened in this business that have been pretty strange. For instance, I'll start out by saying, no, I haven't been satisfied. But you don't have any more studios, you see? There's no such thing as a studio business these days. They're all independents, and for the most part they're being run by people who weren't in the business last year. They don't know anything. The most available commodity in this business is actors, and they've gotten to the point now, when they have a small budget, they'll pay the money for maybe two or three stars in the movie. And very often now, I think—rather than hire a known, reputable character actor—they'll film in some place like Texas and hire local people out of little theater for two hundred and fifty dollars a week. That's why some of these movies are so damn *bad*.

"Look at an English movie, even an English movie made today. Every part, down to the slightest walk-on, is polished to perfection. But you've got any number of pictures out right now where you'll see they used either stuntmen—this is nothing against stuntmen, most of them just aren't actors—but they'll use either stuntmen or local people in parts that *cry out* for some character actor. Except that a character actor of that caliber can't really make a living these days. There used to be people who did three-day parts, two-day parts ... and they were *good!* You don't have any of those people any more because they can't make a living. So companies just grab whatever they think is right for the part, and they wind up either having to loop the lines or drop the scene."

Granting him his charge that, as average quality goes, these were not Hollywood's golden years, I asked if the public could do anything to influence producers to upgrade their efforts. "They don't really shoot movies any more from the standpoint of what the public likes," Askew replied, "because they have no *contact* with the public. They don't know *anything* about what the public thinks or likes, and don't really *care*. This business is based mainly on distribution. The *making* of a movie is a very small part of the total effort.

"And it's not just producers. Writers, directors, and most actors are totally separated from the public at large. They very seldom *pay* to go see a movie. Everybody goes to see a screening or a preview, and you're sitting in the middle of four hundred people from Hollywood who haven't *paid* to see a movie in *ten years*.

"You *have* to be totally conversant with these things," he roused, "the *reasons* why things are done in this business, because you *can't* let yourself be disillusioned. It is a *business*. It's called, by most of the people in it, 'The Industry' ... so, they may as well be talking about Lockheed."

"Isn't there *any* magic in it for you?" I fished. "Anything about your toil in a fantasy factory that awes you in some way?"

"It's like you asking me the question about 'Porky Pig'," Askew said after a thoughtful pause. "That was just me and Peter and Dennis, who are very good friends, sitting around a fire getting loaded and saying the kind of stuff we might ordinarily say under any circumstances. A lot of times things like that happen in a picture. They don't mean a lot to you. Kind of a repartee that you toss around with friends; and then, because it's isolated on a big screen, I guess it means something to people that it never meant in the beginning. It never crossed my mind that anybody would ever think about that when I did it ... and I've been asked about that line *thousands* of *times*. And it didn't mean a thing to *me*, but it evidently meant *something* to each one of those thousand people. *That's* kind of weird to me, that any little thing you say and do can be amplified into something of utmost importance that really wasn't, to begin with." [June 1976.]

The contrast between jovial, high-spirited Bill McKinney and his malevolent screen personas is a difference of day and night. For his most repugnant transformation, the Georgia mountain man in *Deliverance*, his light brown hair was darkened. "Everything was black, dark," he recalled to me. The shirt was black. His face bristled with dark stubble. His pearly whites wore "tartar," a glutinous liquid makeup applied after each meal to maintain a look of dental neglect. Of the cinematographers he added, "They can do just about anything they want to with a camera." They recorded his five foot 11 inch, 170 pound frame as if it had the bulk of an apish mauler. His brief performance in *Deliverance* still ranks with the most harrowing footage ever shot for the movies, and four years later, at the time we spoke, McKinney said he was still being hired on the strength of it.

Bill McKinney villains have been so eminent as to face two of America's favorite giantkillers. While as "Cobb" he only played the local bully and a bad example for Carson City's youth, he was dispatched by no less than John Wayne in *The Shootist*. For *The Outlaw Josey Wales* he was Captain Terrill, a Quantrill-style irregular who wrought pillage and indiscriminate slaughter on behalf of the Union. At the movie's opening his raiders murdered Wales' family and torched his farmstead. Wales joined Confederate guerrillas, and after Appomattox became a fugitive from false charges and scalawag justice. Pursued from Missouri to Texas, the Clint Eastwood hero locked his old enemy in mortal hand-to-hand in the final sequence. The camera closed in as Wales wrung Terrill's sword arm. With only the two heads framed in extreme close-up, blood began to stream from Terrill's mouth. The camera pulled back from his bearded, ursine face to show that Wales had skewered him, apparently, with Terrill's own saber. He sank to the ground, the weapon still protruding front and back, thrust in a steep diagonal through his body. Justice, however, turned a blind eye to the character McKinney jokingly dubbed his "favorite role." As Art he sauntered wordlessly through *The Parallax View*, assassinating politicos, co-conspirators, and seekers of truth. Director Alan Pakula isolated McKinney in the sheer knowledge that he was playing a killer, and talked him through his scenes enough to indicate the target and method of murder. Without ever seeing a script, McKinney enacted a flawless, chilling mime.

Occasionally a villain is there not as a dastard, but for the laughs; in which capacity McKinney has displayed a superb flair for comedy. In a television film *The West, How It Really Was*, he bore a grudge with (not yet "Wild") Bill Hickock, and cornered the easygoing cowboy in a hotel room. Needing to kill him quietly, McKinney gravely considered aloud, "Ah guess'll hafta *beat*'cha to day-uth." In *For Pete's Sake* he portrayed Rocky, a cattle rustler, somewhat incongruous in the New York environs wearing a bandoleer and brandishing a Winchester rifle. For *Cannonball* he was the roughneck driver Cade Redmond, and a belly laugh as he raced his machine across the country badmouthing his passengers, and cackling maniacally as his dirty tricks scratched unsuspecting competitors. Stopping for provisions at a small store along the way, he guzzled a bottle of favorite sustenance and eulogized, "A-a-a-ah, beer! The *bes'* way to gitcha vitee-mins. Better'n spinach. Better'n furrburgers! Better'n ... *possum!*" Although Redmond met a villain's death, McKinney stirred more laughter and garnered more interest than *Cannonball*'s title character and star. For *Thunderbolt and Lightfoot* he embodied an early phantasm of *Deer Hunter* director Michael Cimino, roaring from nowhere in a haze of hydrocarbons with a birdcaged raccoon beside him and a trunkful of squeaking bunnies for live target practice.

Conversations between strangers generally begin with some hesitancy on both sides, but when McKinney discovered his interviewer was Tennessee-born like himself, an air of formality lifted, and soon we were knocking about in a common idiom. Traces of his native Chattanooga still colored his speech as he told in a rich, sonorous, expensively trained voice how he had always wanted to be an actor. Much as he has studied since confirming that hope, he stubbornly resisted early education, dropping from high school, but finally getting an equivalence certificate in the Navy. Even at the Pasadena Playhouse, which he joined after discharge, he recoiled from scripts normally considered first rate material—Shakespeare. "Fifteen years ago when I was goin' to school," he said, "they wanted to push it on me then. I said, 'Shit, man! Get that crap outta here! I don't wanta read that stuff!' I thought it was just a buncha goddamn words." Now with the Actors' Studio, McKinney often rehearses a piece from the Bard. "You know, he ain't hard to understand. It's another thing to do it well, but Shakespeare, man, he knew *exactly* what *he* was doin'. That cat was a good writer. He just painted all of his characters in words." Still, for actual book work, McKinney admits a distaste. "I don't *care* about academics. I never *have* cared about academics. I'm a field man. I like to learn on the job. I like to talk to people that know things, and get from *them*." Because of Pasadena Playhouse's reputation as the training ground for many prominent actors, I remarked how he seemed to have chosen one of the best places for that level of instruction. "Well," he said, "not really. It's a good school, I'd say that; but then you'll always find that your institutions are lacking. It was good as far as learning fundamentals, but any kind of art's a tricky thing. The best way—I'll go back to what I said before—is rather than do the academics of it, if you could *apprentice* with somebody that knows ... that's the best way to learn anything. They can tell you in an *hour* what you can learn in *months* of book learning, or maybe *never* learn it.

"It's been hit-and-miss," he said of his career. "I've been in and out of the business, you know. I started over fifteen years ago. I did tree surgery and stuff like that to keep on takin' singin' lessons and actin' lessons, and keep on eatin'. That's the way it is. It takes a long time, man."

The voice lessons served a duel purpose, one to satisfy a love for music, another to expand McKinney's employability. He claimed a specialty in "blue light" music, a sophisticated mix of jazz, show tunes, blues, uptown country. He mapped out a strategy of acquiring exposure by bringing his music to television as a talk show guest; not as a movie bad guy, but as Bill McKinney the singer. The novelty would hit when his credits were mentioned *after* he had "laid out" a song. "That's what I would like to do," he mused. "That's a vague plan, you know. It's not a specific plan, but that's a good idea."

"What else does it take to get established?" I asked. "Will you be looking for more sympathetic parts?"

"I don't want to limit myself," he answered. "I don't care anything about doin' romantic leads all the time, and I don't want to do just shit-kickers all the time, either. I'd like to mix it up. I like to be a working actor, and do good parts, and the recognition will come. The *work* is the main thing," he stressed, "the effort you put out day-to-day, and the tenacity. It's not the talent that establishes most people. It's the *work*. It really is, because there's a lot of people in the business that just have a minimal amount of talent ... but a great *desire*. They'll work their fannies off to get the thing done. You have your great talents, too, like Brando. But he also works his ass off. He's a hard worker. A lot of stars are hard workers, and that's why they're there.

"I've worked with some very experienced actors. That's helped me a lot ... and observin' people, and life in general, because that's what you're doin'. If you can't make it live, if you can't show a piece of life when you're up there workin', you may as well quit. An actorish actor," he qualified, "is *not* goin' to be a *star*. People are not goin' to relate to 'im. John Wayne, Clint Eastwood, Chuck Bronson — all these people are not actorish actors — Jimmy Stewart, you go right down the line ... Ward Bond ... *all* these people. People out there in the world identify with 'em. They say, 'Yeah, man. Yeah! *I* know that. *I've* felt like that. *I* see things that way.' That's also why these guys are where they are. If a person has a tendency to be actorish, then he might make a livin' in the field, but he'll never be a star because people won't identify with 'im. That's where *that's* at."

"Tell me about that graphic homosexual rape scene in *Deliverance*," I said. "As much as it's boosted your career, it had to be one of the most difficult things you've ever done."

"I'll tell you what it amounted to is, say, a day of hard work," he stated matter-of-factly. "I've been asked that before, how it affected me emotionally and psychologically, and I said, 'Man, *I* don't know. That sounds like a headshrink question.' I told 'em I had an experience when I was a kid. I moved from Tennessee to Georgia, and I was the *new* kid, you know, and these guys used to beat me up and they'd humiliate me ... so, I just turned this thing around and I used that. The hate ... and I used his bein' from the city and havin' more money and havin' a smart mouth and all that, and I used hate in humiliatin' him. In that way, it wasn't a homosexual act per se, as much as it was an act of just complete contempt and humiliation. Of course, the term 'homosexual' is valid, because that could be there. He *could* have been, but as far as in my mind when *I* played it, all I focussed on was the hate and contempt and bullying of this man, and the mastery over 'im. I had 'im under complete control."

"It was certainly a shocker," I observed. "So violent, in fact, as to draw a restricted rating. Eventually your young son will be able to see it, at least on television if you don't accompany him to a theater before he's eighteen. Are you concerned about the impressions it will make when he sees his father that way?"

"Shoot, I don't care," McKinney said, unruffled. "I'll tell you what! We're *close*, and that son of mine will be able to handle *Deliverance* by the time he's *three years old*. You know, he's strong. He's a strong boy, and I'm teaching him *values*! I've taught 'im values from the *day* he could understand *anything*. I'd go into 'im every mornin' and make 'im laugh. I'd try to get 'im to laugh and see the humor in life, and that life was good, and fear was not a great thing; that it's better to be strong and happy and think of life as a privilege, rather than fear, and all that. So I think he can handle *Deliverance*, yeah."

McKinney spoke from the solid stuff he was made of. It was not a prude's testimony nor a witless lowbrow's; but his positive nature did place a limit on what he could tolerate in the name of art. At the one point in our interview during which he sounded genuinely rancorous, McKinney lashed out at the spinelessness of a film he had recently seen, Ingmar Bergman's *Face to Face*. "I *hated* that thing, man," he spat. "Bergman's a tremendous director. The guy knows what motion pictures are all about: a minimum of dialogue, a maximum of good head shots, good facial reactions … very graphic. He's terrific, and that's what offended me. The guy is so capable of doing some great work, and he did not. He puts out a piece of trash like that, a big piece of self-indulgence on his part and on the part of Liv Ullman. That's my opinion, you know. It really got me hot under the collar.

"Let me tell you: I saw my grandmother die. She was a great woman. She told us she was goin' to die two years before it happened. She called her shot, man. She told me two years before, she said, 'I'm not afraid to die.' She'd always been a hard-workin' woman, very strong, so I wasn't surprised that she went out like that. But it made me feel good that she handled it that way.

"*Face to Face* enraged me. It made me so mad that this good director and good actress… I hated it. I *hated* it! There was so much *whining* about pain and death and depression and all that. A piece of junk. A piece of crap! I couldn't stand it. Terrible!"

"I'm sure you'll agree," I said, "that one area where Bergman has excelled is in presenting the surreal. You've made your own foray into that region with the 'Crazy Driver,' a bizarre, flipped-out cameo for *Thunderbolt and Lightfoot*. Whose invention was that? Did you improvise, or was he all spelled out for you?"

"Oh, I improvised quite a bit on that," he brightened, his anger at the nihilism of *Face to Face* quickly subsiding. "The character reminded me — there, again — of a guy I knew in Georgia. He talked with a cleft palate, and the first time they got in the car, Eastwood and Jeff Bridges, I said, 'You know somethin', man? This reminds me of a guy I used to live across the street from and … 'e taw' lah' thisz…' and I did that cleft palate talk. Eastwood says, 'Jesus Christ, that would be great to do the part like that!' That shot was not a take anyway, so we asked the director if it would work out. He was kind of afraid of it, but he said try it. I jus' started doin' that, and he never said anything else about it, so I played the whole part that way. It added more to it, I think, 'cause this guy was really crazy...

"Another thing, too—the exhaust pipes up through the floor. That made it all kinda crazy, because Cimino was sayin', 'Well, maybe there's kind of a sexual overtone here. This guy, he picks up two guys that are kinda' nice lookin', and he's tryin' to gas *them*, and see if *they* can last as long as *he* can, and maybe he gets his *jollies* that way.' Also, shootin' the rabbits. It was kinda weird. But all in all, it came off funny. That whole thing, we did that interior driving scene where I'm in the car sayin', 'Geh 'n the back, geh 'n the back. Ah gah no leg'l ob'gation. Ah go aw ovuh the country—eas' coas', wes' coas', in'where you waw go!' That was all improvisation. We just got in the car and *shot* the goddamn thing.

"And the point of it is, it was not part of the story at all. It was just out of left field. The writer/director, Mike Cimino, told me that when I first saw it. We did it, and he saw the scene when it was cut, and liked it; but said, 'I can't understand why everybody is laughin' at that scene!' I said, 'Jesus Christ, man. You said it was funny, to go ahead.' He said, 'Yeah, but I still can't understand it.'"

My next query proved to be a simplistic one, as McKinney laughed outright when asked if he used *The Method*. "Okay, I tell you," he chuckled. "I never try to pre-guess it. I just go in empty. I don't set up any kind of rigid framework to go by. I'm a member of the Actors' Studio, and in answer to your question, I don't use any particular 'method.' The only method that I do use is to stay as loose as possible and as flexible as possible, and work within that.

"When I work, I just read the script over quite a few times and do some thinkin' about it and get the interrelationships of the characters, and that's the technical part of it. But when it comes down to rollin' the camera, then whatever happens happens. I just let the song lay out, just let it play the way it plays ... and that's the way it happens. Breath to breath ... moment to moment. I don't want to work the same thing twice. I don't believe in that. If it's gonna be creative, then it has to be fresh. What might work one time won't work the next time.

"See, a lot of guys go for that *Deliverance* quality, and they miss it. I've been hired a lot of times to reproduce a quality like that; but the thing that they don't understand is the director and the conditions that existed at the *moment*. When you get before a camera... I'll give you an example. The wind might be blowin', the sun might be hot, it might be snowin'— God knows *what* the hell's goin' to happen—but you've got a *scene* to shoot. Now, under those conditions, you might be able to take this script and read it in a room and have certain ideas, but under those outside conditions, *other* things happen to you—physically, emotionally, mentally. Your blood pressure might go up. It might go down. *All* this shit. So, you are really, very definitely affected.

"You can't put it under a glass, man! It has to *happen*. With *Deliverance*, John Boorman made it happen, and *we* made it happen, and the *location* made it happen." McKinney cited *The Outfit* in which he had a belligerent walk-on role: "They wanted another *Deliverance* kind of thing, and it just don't work out that way. I saw it, and I said, 'Well, I was standin' there talkin', and it was all right, and it was conversational, but it wasn't really that good.' Not my part. It was okay."

"Do you take any special approach to playing a *heavy*, though?" I asked. "For example, I've read of one actor whose firm conviction in the existence of evil—he claimed—had powered several of his villainous roles."

"I don't know what this actor means about 'the existence of evil,' whether he's just talkin' about common evil, or whether he's talkin' about demons or what, or *both*; but if that works for 'im, man, that's fine. That's his motor. *I* know there's evil, and I know there's *good* ... but I really can't say," he spoke almost mystically, "I can't really pinpoint what I use, and I don't even know if I want to. I just seem to have a lot of fuel to use. Those things *came* to me when I did *Deliverance*. All of a sudden it came to me that when I lived in Georgia these guys used to whack on me and beat me up, throw my bike in the creek, and all that stuff ... and I said, 'Wow! Yeah!' The memory came back, just like it was recorded. It might have been from Actors' Studio training that I did remember that, but I find that things do come to you if you don't push too hard for 'em. And that's how it is in life. If you push too hard for things, they seem to evade you.

"Whether they work out well or not is a matter of conjecture, but things do seem to come to me, just *pre*-thought out. What I'm sayin' is that I cannot tell you any kind of method or anything that has influenced me, as far as acting goes. It's like what Jack Dempsey said about fights, man. When it comes down to it, if you can do it at 8:30 in the Garden on such-and-such a night, you can *do* it ... and that's what I think about acting."

"What kind of treatment does a character actor usually get from the big stars?" I asked. "You had a small scene in *For Pete's Sake* with Barbra Streisand, a superstar with quite a take-charge reputation. Did you ever feel condescended to, or see any fits of star temperament?"

"No indeed!" McKinney disputed. "No, not at all. We got along very well, I felt. She seemed quite nice, and easy to work with. I've worked with Raquel Welch, too, and a lot of people claimed to have trouble with her, and I never did. I've really had a good *rapport* with people. But ... I never have really been in *awe* of anybody, that I can remember. Now, I did a job for Igor Stravinsky one time, man, and *this* cat's probably the heaviest cat I'll ever meet in my *life*. I did this job for 'im when I was doin' tree work, and boy, this cat was *really heavy*. You knew you were really talkin' to somebody. And when he took your hand, you knew you had a holda somethin' with some *energy* in it. I've *yet* to find anybody that could match *him*, as far as impressing me as a person. But what people do for a livin' and how successfully they do it, why, that's either their fortune or misfortune. The only single thing that impresses me about somebody is *them*. I either like 'em or don't like 'em, or agree with 'em, or don't agree with 'em."

"In an industry where not that many Southerners are highly visible or prominent, does being a Southerner carry a stigma? You not only play a lot of Southerners," I noted, "but you *are* one. Are you ever dealt with less fairly, or less cordially because of this?"

"Well, I pretty much write people off," he replied. "I mean, I don't believe in that kinda shit. But if somebody's gonna do that, I say, 'Well, fuck you *too*, man!' That's *my* attitude."

"You've done some television," I commented, "in fact, you had a recurrent role as sheriff in *The Family Holvak*. Its purported setting was in Tennessee which, by the way, you and I know doesn't anywhere resemble the landscape where *Holvak* was filmed. Those were the same California hills Hopalong Cassidy galloped through. I half expected clumps of sagebrush occasionally to blow across those 'Tennessee' roads. At any rate, what's your attitude towards television work? A fill-in between movie jobs? Would you do another series?"

"Television needs actors to fill specific demands. Like for *Holvak* they needed a guy to play a Tennessee sheriff, and I fit the order.

"But the reason that I really don't care for television," he said more heatedly, "is that they're really not in the entertainment medium, as such, as they are for sellin' soap and brassieres. Just like ... movies are in the entertainment medium, and so are nightclubs and places like that; but television — they got captive trade, man! You buy a television set, and you turn the sumbitch on an' *watch* it! For that reason, they have sagebrush on *Holvak*. They don't give a shit — you know? — not that much. They don't care about whether things are authentic that much or not. They want to sell frick and frack. Anyway, a series'd just be tyin' me down. I'm not sayin' I *wouldn't* do one. I just take it as it comes, but I sure ain't *lookin'* for one."

"Are the financial rewards an important concern to you whenever you consider a new job?"

"Financial reward means a *hell* of a lot to me, not only for the *money*," he contended, "but for the fact of how people *think* of you, people in the *industry*.

"I don't put any limit onto what I intend to make. I'm gettin' more money all the time, and I'm on an upward trend. I just figure as long as I follow my game plan to a certain extent and keep those things goin', and if

God means for it to happen, or the powers-that-be mean for it to happen, it'll *happen*. And if it don't ... *I* ain't gonna *shoot* myself. I'll jus' keep livin' my life."

Obviously 15 years of ins and outs had not scrambled Bill McKinney's priorities in life as a family man, nor blunted his optimism as a professional, and an actor eager to prove his versatility. Cheerfully he reiterated his grand scheme: "And see, that's one thing singin' will do for me. That'll get me off the *heavy* shit. If you can show people that you have some kind of sensitivity, and *do* it — I mean, not just *tell* 'em about it, but *do* it — then people will say, 'Jesus Christ, man, the cat can sing a song! He's got *feelings!* That country redneck can *sing*, he's got *feelings!*"

Q.E.D. [April 1976.]

IV

Inspector Callahan's Nemesis

"The Great White Way"—Off Broadway—O.O.B.—"Tony"—
"Obie"—Simon—Nichols—Papp ... et cetera, et cetera. This is name-dropping on a grand scale. No theatrical venture is more legitimate than one taking place within the province of "the New York stage," a collective entity with a reputation unchallenged in the Western Hemisphere. "The New York stage" dazzles without tinsel. It is the real thing. Atop a pyramid of directors, writers, actors, designers, and acting, dance and music schools anywhere, that small fraction of the whole that is associated with the New York stage forms the apex, and enjoys the lion's share of prestige. Of the millions in the U.S.A. viewing all stage, film and television productions, the comparative handful who are New York theater patrons are counted first among the truly blessed. In an age of skepticism, is it safe to ask: Can anything be *that* good?

The answer to this gauche conjecture, even after discounting a certain measure of Gothamite boosterism, is: Yes, possibly so. Impeccable credentials from the most "legitimate" source are no guarantee of success in Hollywood, but the fact remains that countless film stars owe their professional baptisms to New York. A discipline acquired in theater work has resulted for them in consistently smooth performances ranging over a wide field of assignments; and Andrew Robinson, another East Coast transferee, has been no exception.

Andrew Robinson has been handy for various television series, played a hillbilly doughboy for the serialized *Once an Eagle*, small-time hoods in *Charley Varrick* and *The Drowning Pool*, even a regular on the popular daytime drama *Ryan's Hope*; but no role has equalled the intensity and power of his Scorpio, the demented sniper of 1971's shock-laden *Dirty Harry*. It may be a tribute to Robinson's creation that a subsequent sniper tale, 1976's *Two Minute Warning*, never offered a sustained view of its own villain's face, only medium to distant shots and rear views showing his curly brown hair and a manner of street dress that were strongly reminiscent of Robinson's Scorpio.

Andrew Robinson graduated with a degree in English from the New School for Social Research and received a Fulbright scholarship to London's Royal Academy of Dramatic Arts before beginning a stage career in New York. By the time we interviewed, however, he had been residing comfortably for several years in Pacific Palisades, California. The change of climate, however, had hardly produced a "laid back" attitude regarding his profession, as he was quick to warn me: "I must say, if this was just a 'Hollywood Confidential' kind of thing, I would somehow try to avoid it."

"Did you always want to be an actor?" I kicked off, after assuring him my intentions were honorable.

"Pretty much. It was when I got a Fulbright scholarship to RADA in London that I really got into it intensively. That was, I guess, about thirteen years ago."

"Southern California is quite a change from either London or New York," I remarked. "Do you like the great outdoors? Are you a hunter? That rifle you used in *Dirty Harry* didn't look like it was in the hands of a novice."

"No, I'm not an outdoors sportsman," Robinson replied, "with *guns*, that is. I'm a tennis player and a runner, things like that. But in terms of the gun stuff, guns have always frightened me, freaked me out. When I went to do *Dirty Harry*, it was with the help of two prop men that got me familiar with all those various guns in the movie. And it was only through my work, my *rehearsing* with those guns that I became comfortable with them and was able to use them as I did in *Dirty Harry*, or in *Charley Varrick*, or any other times that I've used a gun."

"So you began as a stage actor?"

"Yeah, I was living in New York and working primarily as a stage actor, and I did, I would say, over fifty plays before I got to *Dirty Harry* and moved out to California. It was while I was doing an adaptation of Dostoevskij's *The Idiot*, which is about this young Russian prince who is a very saintly person. He's an epileptic, and very outgoing and generous and kind in a society where that's considered an aberration, and where he's considered an idiot for these saintly qualities. So that's when I met Don Siegel, and Clint Eastwood came to the show, and I was hired for *Dirty Harry*."

"Suddenly you're a movie star."

"Well," Robinson replied hesitantly, "it was one of those flukes, I guess, where you'd say that I was so-called discovered ... although that always cracks me up when an actor who's been around a while and has done a lot of work is suddenly 'discovered.'

"Anyway, they came to see the show. At least, Clint did. I met Don for just fifteen or twenty minutes, and I thought there was no future with this because he was in town for only a short time, and wasn't able to watch me in the play. But then, Clint did; and I found myself with the job playing the psychopathic killer opposite Clint Eastwood in a Don Siegel directed Hollywood movie. I had to be in San Francisco in a week from the time that I heard I was hired."

"I must say," I declared, "I don't believe I have ever seen any film so tightly produced to move an audience to outrage as *Dirty Harry* did. It was super box office, and top ten in the Nielsens its first two times on television. Now, big box office doesn't necessarily indicate quality; but I am amazed that *Dirty Harry* received little, if any, critical acclaim for some of the picture's obvious merits. Practically everything about it was top-notch — the acting, the photography, the editing — all under the superb direction of Don Siegel. As well as I can ascertain, however, critics wrote it off as a routine cop/sniper shootout, casually tossing out terms like 'fascist' and 'macho' to denigrate it."

"That is a rather typical popular opinion held by certain of the critics who — ... They like to have their good and their bad guys clearly defined; in other words, so that they can be on the side of someone who's clearly opposing, you know, the fascist, murderous, bad people.

"I think what Don Siegel did was that subliminally, subconsciously, he set it up so that Harry was just as much of a fascist and just as much of a killer as the sniper, Scorpio. So that kind of screwed people's minds around a bit. They didn't know who was good and who was bad," Robinson said. "Plus, the subject matter of the film *was* fascist, and it was *disturbing*, so that people just wrote it off as a sort of fascist cop/sniper shootout. Which it was, but it *was* magnificently produced; and Siegel brought out all of his considerable skills and experience in this movie and, I feel, brought a mediocre script and raised it to a very high level. As a matter of fact, it broke ground in terms of genre, because it combined a number of genres. It combined the cowboy, the Western showdown; the cops and robbers; and it also added the horror film element. It successfully merged all these three."

"Your performance was so electrifying," I said, "I was surprised that it did not at least attract a Best Supporting Actor Oscar nomination."

"Since you mentioned it," Robinson admitted, "I fully expected to be nominated for an Academy Award for that; and I must say, *no* one is a more harsh critic on my work than I am. When I remember what the character was on paper, he was described as middle-aged, balding, paunchy; somebody, you know, who I guess I've seen hanging around bus terminals in Chicago or New York or any place. And when Siegel and I started working on it, and how we built that character. I must say, 'how he *allowed* me,' because the director really, once he gets into the filming, has too many things to do than to start helping an actor create a role. The actor really has to do that himself. That's why it's so extraordinarily important that the director cast a role correctly. Siegel's great genius and the beauty of working with him is that he allowed me the freedom to make my choices, as long as I got behind them a hundred percent, and as long as they didn't rip up the script or distort the story as it's written ... because it's a very simple story. There's no psychological delving into the why's and wherefore's.

"But that doesn't make any difference, that doesn't bother me. For instance, that Kezar Stadium scene, I watched that on television, and this occurred to me: Any amount of psychological delving into, or explaining what his *mother* did to him, or what his *father* did to him, what his *environment* was, would not match up to just that emotional spectacle of that man on the ground in that stadium, going through those incredible changes and… I mean, that told me a *world* about that character. I didn't *need* any textbook to explain what his character was about. I *knew* what that character was about from that scene, and indeed from a couple of other places. So, because I felt I had done my work as an actor successfully, and because it was a very sensational kind of role, I thought, 'Well, *by God!*,' you know? 'Like … uh … I should be up for an *award*.'

"I wasn't. I wasn't even nominated. But since then," Robinson added, "since it was my first movie and I was really rather naive, I realize that you get awards — and I think this applies to any situation — from a *backlog*. It's a *body* of work. Jack Nicholson finally gets it for *Cuckoo's Nest*. Although I thought he was wonderful in it, he was equally wonderful in any of his other movies. But, it's finally because it was a backlog of work. And it's all very political and all that, so … that's okay."

"The exposure you got from *Dirty Harry* generated a lot more work for you, didn't it?" I asked.

"The problem was, that people wanted to typecast me as this killer," he said heatedly. "Indeed, they did. And it's been very difficult for me, because I want to play the range. My talent is such that I can play a wide range of people; but because they see this overwhelming person, this 'Scorpio' killer on the big screen, this is what happens in the film business. It doesn't happen in stage. In stage you can play one character, and then you get offered another character, and you run the gamut. But in films, it's different. It seems like an image burns in the people's heads, and it takes them a long time to get through it. So only now am I finally getting through it, although my reputation is an excellent one, and an excellent one as a heavy … which is fine, you know. Most of my heroes in films have been heavies. And most of the really good roles are heavies… So, that's okay. But I'm finding I'm finally getting to a range; although to make a living I've had to play some rather stupid psychopathic types, like for television, but *that's* okay. That's been like a workshop for me, a *film* workshop. Film has different demands from stage, so I needed a place to work out, and television has been a fine place for me to learn."

"Would you say you more or less carried the character of Scorpio inside you while doing him," I asked, "or was he merely an external creation? And where did you draw him from? Did you use any models from real life, or perhaps from literature? A Raskolnikov with a Springfield and scope?"

"I love that … Raskolnikov," Robinson said, laughing, "considering that it was Dostoevskij that got me into this *Dirty Harry* thing to begin with.

"Yeah, you know, my feeling is if you're an actor worth your salt, with *any* character, but *especially* with something like *Dirty Harry*, you really do have to go through such emotional extremes in order to make it believable. I think that's the actor's job. You really have to be a believable character so that the audience can take the trip, not just *indicate* the character. You can't fool anyone. No one is really, truly going to get involved with you if you're just indicating what the character is about. By 'indicating,' I mean, say with Scorpio if I just sort of ranted and raved, but went through none of the emotional changes or, as they say, 'internalized' the character of Scorpio, which is like ... that's what I did. He was both an external and an internal creation. It's like hooking up with one's own demons, so to speak, if you're playing someone who is controlled by his demons. Most of us are in control of our little box of demons. So as an actor, you experiment and find out what it is to be controlled *by* your demons. What I mean is, internally I had to make this connection to all the rage and anger and frustration that I feel or have ever felt in my own life. By making that connection with *my* anger, *then* I was able to 'put on the costume,' the external trappings of this character; the gun, the laugh, the twisted face, the broken teeth ... all those things that are *not* me. And by making the connections between the internal and the external, you have the character of Scorpio. Now, this is easier said than done, of course. This is what one calls 'acting technique,' and this is what I've spent a lot of time doing. This is my work in life, my craft.

"There's a lot of glossy, indicated acting in television, by the way, which I'm not putting down," Robinson insisted, "because there's room for that. You've got to have it all so that we can put the various forms in perspective. Like, *Dirty Harry* would've been just another TV movie—which I felt like its sequel was, *Magnum Force*—but Don Siegel brought *Dirty Harry* and lifted it right out of the mundane, pedestrian levels to a real piece of dramatic art."

"I've read of older stars taking younger ones under wing," I said, "sharing their knowledge of acting. Your films have put you on the set not only with Eastwood and Matthau, but with some very fine supporting players. Did working with these film people prove to be instructive?"

"I have worked with a lot of really very fine actors," Robinson answered readily, "but it's not so much a case of older actors taking younger ones under wing. No one's ever took *me* under their wing. It's not because people are paranoid, or there's competition or whatever. It's just that there's not really time. But what happens is that you can learn just simply by watching, certainly by acting with people.

"Clint is not an actor. Clint is a very strong *presence*. Clint does what he does, and does it very well; but he's not an actor. He would never pretend to be an actor. He gets out there and he just tries to fill the moment with his presence, and it's a very *strong* presence.

"Matthau is an actor; and working with him, I learned something

Andrew Robinson 85

else. With Clint, I learned something about presence and about fulfilling yourself for a moment and just *being there.* Matthau ... you learn something about acting, and let's say, he was more helpful. But Walter's a more outgoing person anyway in working with you. And all the other people I've worked with, I've seen how it's their wealth of experience that gives them extra-added dimension when you see them on screen."

"I happened to catch you in the PBS production of Arthur Miller's *Incident at Vichy*, also starring Harris Yulin, Richard Jordan, Bert Freed, René Auberjenois, and Alan Garfield," I said. "As an acting situation, I assume that effort was equally rewarding. In terms of money; if work in films and commercial TV is more lucrative, could you *afford* to turn those assignments down in order to devote time to something like *Vichy*?"

"It was wonderful," said Robinson. "Almost all of them are good friends, like Harris Yulin and Richard Jordan, René Auberjenois — very, very close friends, and excellent actors. And it was wonderful to be able to work with that kind of material, Miller's play, and with these people. It was doing a stage play on film, with Stacy Keach, who is an excellent director. He got us all together, and we had a proper rehearsal time, like a couple of weeks to rehearse on this so we could find more depth and more character, and we had a great time.

"Television... You can make a few bucks in television so that you can *afford* to do something like *Vichy*, which is like, you know, for almost no money at all. This is one of the things in this commercial, capitalistic system that an actor — if he wants to continually challenge him- or herself — has to arrange, to get those commercial money gigs so that you *can* afford to work for nothing. I did a play in L.A. by David Story, an English playwright, called *The Changing Room.* It's about an English rugby team, and none of us were getting any money for it. But it was our workshop. We were learning a few things about ourselves and our business. And I did a two-hour movie for NBC called *Lannigan's Rabbi* with Art Carney and Stu Margolin. The character I played was a very nice character; but other than being a little different and an interesting character to play, basically it was not that challenging. But it enabled me to not only do *The Changing Room*, but I went to New York to do a play at Joe Papp's theater — the same theater where I had done Dostoevskij's *Idiot* — and it was not much money. I broke even, because I had to go there and my family had to stay in LA. because my wife was in a play at Ralph Waite's theater, and I broke even. In terms of the economics, that's how one has to sort of work it."

"You've done quite a number of heavy roles for film and especially television. Is there something inherent you have that qualifies you for that?"

"Well, no. There's nothing about me that 'inherently qualifies' me for the lot of the villain. Someone once told me," he joked, "my 'intense blue eyes.'

"See," he continued, now serious, "Don Siegel hired me to play Scorpio because he wanted someone that *didn't* look like a psychopathic killer, and I *don't*. I'm 35-years-old, I look about 25-years-old, and old ladies dote on me. And there's nothing ... even my bad temper is now mellowed out, I've finally got control of that.

"And I'm not in a mold," he insisted. "It's not that I'm trapped. I *used* to feel trapped, perhaps; but I don't feel trapped anymore. I feel like I can do anything, and it's a wonderful feeling of freedom, too. I can choose or not choose to do any job that I want. There are commercial considerations, of course, when you have a family. I'm married to a beautiful woman and an actress, Irene, and we have a little girl, Rachel. But still, I don't feel that there's any mold that I have to break out of."

"What other actors or actresses do you especially admire?"

"I thought Nicholson's work was masterful in *One Flew Over the Cuckoo's Nest*. He's a wonderful actor. Of course, Brando never ceases to inspire. And there are other people, too, like Gene Hackman. I love his energy and his integrity, even when he's in a lousy movie, like I thought *French Connection II* was. He has a couple of scenes, for instance when he's coming off dope and he's going through the whole baseball trip; and he's this lonely cop in Marseilles, and he goes into the bar and has that thing with the bartender. I mean, those two moments take that lousy movie and elevate it to something else.

"I like a lot of people. I like anyone who works and tries to relate something about their own life. They are expressing some sense of themselves in each role, and doing it with as much integrity and honesty and energy that they are able to at the time. Like the friend of mine who's making it now — and I'm really glad he is, because he's a wonderful actor — Bobby DeNiro. He's another one I like. A couple of other people I can think of that I really enjoyed working with ... well, Art Carney. He's a genius! From his head to his toes, the man is just wonderful; wonderful when the camera's running, and when the camera's not running. He's just a genuinely inventive, real person. And Cloris Leachman, whom I did a TV movie with called *Someone I Touched* that I really liked. There are *lots* of good actors, actresses around; so many, I mean, you can't even start talking about them. And it's when the material starts getting better, especially for women, that we'll start seeing a lot more people who really have something to say."

"When you're out in public," I asked, "what kind of feedback do you get on some of your heavy characters?"

"Sometimes people in the street will see me — it used to happen a lot," Robinson recalled, "when *Dirty Harry* was creating its splash — and people would not immediately put me together with the film ... and they would just kind of *freak*! One woman in this doctor's office came over to me and said, 'Listen, I'm sorry.' I said, 'What are you sorry about?' and she said, 'When you came into the office, I immediately hated you.' And I felt this, just like I'm sensitive to this now, but sensitive to the point where I just detach myself, I no longer get involved with it. When it first started happening, though, it would freak *me* out. I would get very uptight. But I knew that this woman was going through all these changes with me, and I said, 'That's okay!' We ended up having a very nice discussion.

"But this happens a lot. A lot of people, you know — and I can relate to this, because that's how I was — a lot of people *relate* to villains, and they relate to the actors that *play* the villains. They know that the actors playing villains are not 'bad' guys, and there's a certain respect, a certain feeling that these people have. *I* was certainly interested in villains, and I still am; because quite frankly, I'll tell you, I think as a rule — this is a generalization — the best actors play the heavies. And the best actors play those characters that are borderline heavies. Hackman, DeNiro, they get into playing those kinds of characters, as Brando does, as even Nicholson does ... any of those guys. Certainly I see how well Eddie Robinson and Bogart did. And there's something a little more at stake, I think, than playing a romantic lead; although God knows if you get an actor who's playing a romantic lead who's honest, and not just walking through it with his best profile, that *too* can be revelatory. But there's something built into the villain where you really are offered the opportunity to expose just a little more of yourself, which for me is always very interesting."

"Most outsiders, in respect to the film industry, envision life in Hollywood as being a stable of fancy cars, opulent houses, parties, an abundance of gorgeous and available women — in short, the image of 'Hollywood Babylon.' How do you, as a relative newcomer to film, relate your life to 'Tinseltown?' You're young enough," I cracked, "to give us the orgiast's-eye-view."

"Hollywood — believe it or not, Bill — is just another town," Robinson replied testily. "When I say 'Hollywood,' I mean Hollywood itself, the town. Most of the studios are in other towns *around* Los Angeles and Hollywood, like in the San Fernando Valley. Most of the time you can look around and you could be anyplace. You could be in Omaha, Hartford, Shreveport, wherever. And it's such a spread-out kind of place, you've got everything here from soup to nuts.

"There's a kind of affluence here, I guess," he conceded. "I have never seen so many expensive cars and big homes, and there're some sections that are quite impressive. But it's *real* here! It's not altogether 'Tinseltown.' I mean, I really don't understand the whole Tinseltown number. Certainly there is an element of fantasy, no doubt, in this kind of business. And certainly everyone all over the world sees movies made in Hollywood. There's a certain kind of projection on people's part as to what this town is about. Like most of my friends, my wife, myself; when we saw movies from Hollywood, we said to ourselves, 'Oh boy! Someday I'm going to go to Hollywood to make movies.' And indeed, some of us *are*

Bill McKinney ("Captain Terrill") hunts *The Outlaw Josey Wales,* **1975.** 89

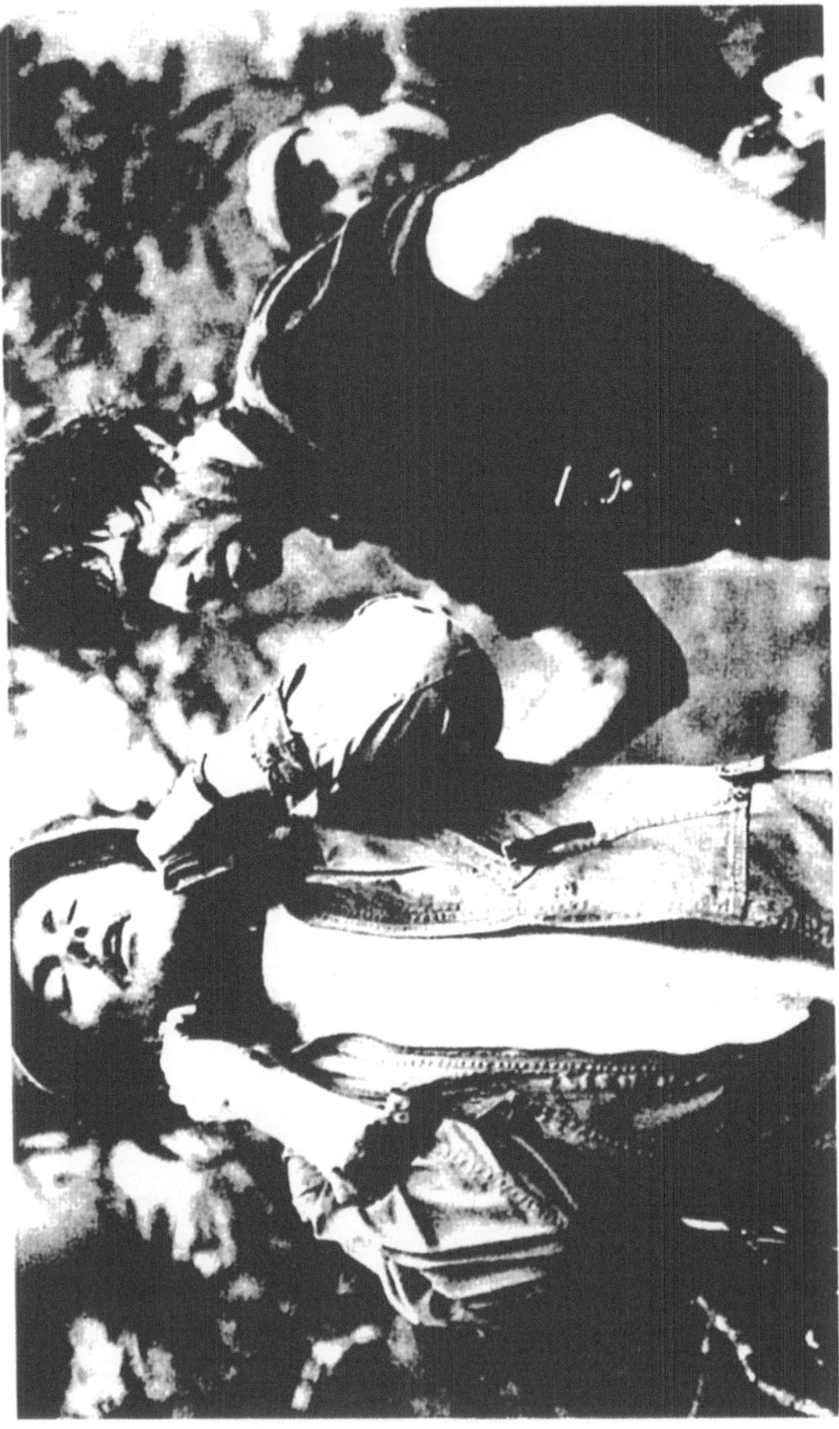

Opposite: Mountain men terrorize a city-bred canoeist in *Deliverance*, 1972; pictured are Jon Voight (left), **Bill McKinney**, Herbert "Cowboy" Coward. Above, top: **McKinney** offscreen. Bottom: "Cade Redmond" (**McKinney**) dims a competitor's hopes of victory in *Cannonball*, 1976.

Opposite, left: *Charley Varrick* (1973) has a criminal accomplice, and Walter Matthau an admiring understudy in **Andrew Robinson**. Right: **Robinson** as "Scorpio," taking aim in *Dirty Harry*, 1971. Above: The mild-mannered exterior Don Siegel sought for his psychotic killer (**Robinson**) in *Dirty Harry*.

 Robert Donner.

"Boss Shorty" (**Donner**) puts leg chains on Paul Newman, *Cool Hand Luke*, 1967.

Opposite: **Robert Donner** (top-hatted) joined Jim Brown, Harry Carey, Jr., Ronald Howard (background), Jim Kelly, Fred Williamson, **Lee Van Cleef**, and Catherine Spaak in *Take a Hard Ride*, 1975. Above, top: **Donner** as a dead-pan villain opposite John Wayne in *El Dorado*, 1967. Bottom: A dapper **Donner** made one of his two romantic conquests on screen in *The Spirit Is Willing*, 1967.

Opposite, top: **L.Q. Jones**. Bottom: **Jones** (left) strings along with Ed Begley and Jonathan Lippe in *Hang 'em High*, 1968. Above: End of the trail for **Jones** in *The Ballad of Cable Hogue*, 1970.

Opposite: front row, from left, Jimmy Shepherd, Paul Harper, Archie Butler; back row, **Strother Martin**, Buck Holland, Robert Ryan, Billy Hart, **L.Q. Jones**, in *The Wild Bunch*, 1969. Above: Ryan may have second thoughts about **Jones** (top) and **Martin** as bunkhouse mates, same movie.

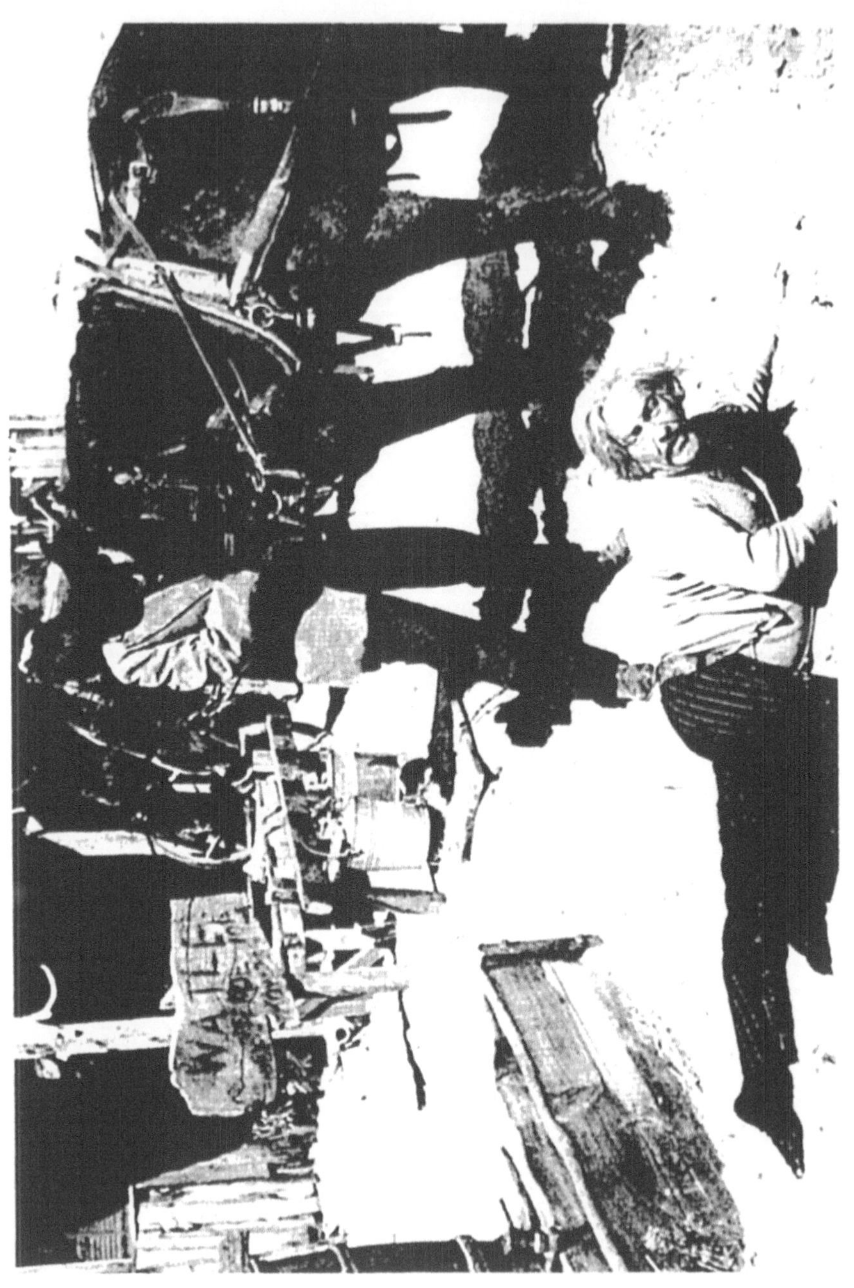

Opposite: **Strother Martin** crawls afeared from a newfangled horseless carriage while Max Evans holds the horses, in *The Ballad of Cable Hogue*, 1970. Above, top: **Martin** (left) grabs a fistful of slither from J.R. Clark in his 1973 star vehicle *Sssssss*. Bottom: In *Hard Times*, 1975, James Coburn (left), **Martin**, Charles Bronson are "Speed," "Doc Poe," and "Chaney": three men scraping a living from fistfights and gambling in Depression-era New Orleans.

Strother Martin resumed a "smell of the stable" role as a kindly horse trainer in *The Champ*, 1979.

here making movies. But it's work time, baby. It is *work!* You get up early. You work *hard.* You have to hustle your ass just to *get* work, and to get the kind of work that you feel is expressive of your life and your needs, not just schlop. And for instance, Nathanael West's novel *Day of the Locust* and Fitzgerald's book *The Last Tycoon* — these books are true reflections of, say, people who have come to Hollywood and who have had their dreams smashed right over their heads and their illusions just ripped away. It's *hard.* It's *very* hard out here. And at the same time, for me the hard work and the difficulty of moving — I was an Easterner all my life until about five years ago — is worth it. There are wonderful opportunities out here. One can live — how shall I put it? — *fully* out here. I know for my kids it's a beautiful place to live. And I have animals, and there is room, sunshine. And since we live near the ocean ... well ... *everything* is close. Everyone lives near the ocean, everyone lives near the mountains, everyone lives near the desert, everyone lives near these redwood forests. It can be *paradise*...

"But I think, in a sense, *any* place can be paradise. When I was living in New York, it was a long time before I thought I'd *ever* leave New York. I was very happy there. I had my trip together there. I was working hard, and I was working well, and New York — which is a very difficult place to live, too — was paying off for me. And when I was a kid growing up in New England, for a time I thought *that* was paradise for me. I thought I would never leave New Hampshire, and that, too, was a difficult place to live; because it's a beautiful place, but it's a *harsh* place in terms of its weather, in terms of its economics. I don't think there are any *easy* places to live."

"How has your career changed you, would you say?"

"It has uprooted me, and moved me to another place a few times," Robinson answered. "I have travelled a great deal, I've seen a lot... But *how* it's changed me is really not easy to say, other than I *am changed.* I guess probably the greatest change has been that I have a lot more responsibility now. My days are totally filled."

"Hasn't your income enabled you to purchase some of those accouterments most people associate with Hollywood actors, though," I pressed. "The cars, the house and the rest?"

"Absolutely, but these are *also* incredible responsibilities. Like, when I was in New York I never had a car. I had no *need* for a car. Suddenly, the need for a *car* here, the need for *two* cars so that your wife and kids don't get stranded when you're off on a job somewhere. Things like that, that's amazing to me. That is just amazing. And that means responsibility because I am terribly aware as well there are times of the year where there's this incredible smog problem caused just by that — the cars! That car ... unchecked, uncared for, *killing* the environment.

"The ownership of land," he went on, "well, that's really a joke. The bank owns the land, and you rent it from the bank. Anyway, it's a joke right back to the Indians when they said, 'Sure! You can buy the Island of Manhattan!' and they're looking at each other and saying, 'Who *are* these weird dudes? They want to *buy* the *land*!

"So, I guess the biggest change for me is that being out here, and through responsibility, I'm truly finding my manhood. And this is all tied up with my work in films, there's no doubt about it. It's because of my work as an actor. And I don't make the separation between my life and my acting. Bill Macy, who is on the TV show 'Maude' — a wonderful actor and a wonderful friend — once was talking about acting. We were doing a play in New York and he was talking just off the top of his head, talking about what it was, for him. He says, 'Well, you know, it's like you're walking down the street. You walk down the street, down the sidewalk, you walk into the building, you walk onto a stage, there's an audience, you walk off the stage, you walk back onto the street' ... and there's a *continuum* he's talking about. It's just the *flow* of *life*. And the people I find that I least respond to in an acting situation are the people who do not *admit* to this flow, to this continuum; who try to control some kind of schizophrenic difference."

"Is it too early to ask what your best piece of work has been?"

"Well, that can be anything. For instance, *Dirty Harry*, of course. And *Charley Varrick*, of course. I feel that they are both really successful characterizations. *Vichy*, I enjoyed doing that.

"But you know?" Robinson considered. "I did a *Streets of San Francisco* that Michael Douglas directed — I think it was the only time he directed, and it was in his last season — and I looked at that; and I was terribly proud of that, if only because episodic television is probably the hardest place to act. The scripts are usually lousy, there's no time, and you don't get much help. So, you have to be very strong in your technique, and resilient as well as strong, and very alive and relaxed. You have to really have your shit together to act successfully and from some kind of honest place on episodic television, those hour TV shows; the *Rookies*, the *Ironsides*, the *S.W.A.T.s* and all that. So that *Streets of San Francisco* I was terribly proud of, because I thought it was a good part, and I was *there*, and I helped to build an interesting character. So, any time I achieve my goal, in any given character, I am proud." [May 1976.]

V

Hell on Horseback

The tranquil mood of "Home on the Range" is somehow alien to the cinematic Old West. Discouraging words around there, words-become-flesh in a mother lode of screen villains. Robert Donner, L.Q. Jones and Strother Martin have been exemplary miners of this Western-rustic vein, and each has his share of glistening nuggets. It is this type of heavy by which Donner, Jones and Martin are most readily identified, and although actually they have played a much wider range of characters, to cite them for their Western roles alone — particularly their most horrendous villains — would not do them an injustice. Robert Donner was grimly laughable in *something big*, and a perfect "black hat" opposing John Wayne in *El Dorado, Rio Lobo* and *Chisum*. L.Q. Jones acted in *The Ballad of Cable Hogue, Hang 'em High, Winterhawk, The Hunting Party*, and *Pat Garrett & Billy the Kid*; and teamed with Strother Martin in characterizations of "T.C." and "Coffer" for *The Wild Bunch*, it is unlikely that either Jones or his colleague will ever again seem so verminous. Martin also appeared in *Cable Hogue*, was memorably nasty in *The Man Who Shot Liberty Valance* and *Hannie Caulder*, suspiciously underhanded in *True Grit* and the contemporary Western *Pocket Money*; and thoroughly misanthropic in *Rooster Cogburn*.

On the other hand, war films like *Battle Cry, The Young Lions, The Naked and the Dead* and *Torpedo Run* outnumber Westerns in L.Q. Jones's early film career, and white-collar criminals like the crooked trucking boss of *White Line Fever* also number among his heavies. Strother Martin and Robert Donner are unforgettable from another modern-set vehicle, *Cool Hand Luke*. Not always a complete villain, the most harmful trait Donner displayed in *Fool's Parade* and *High Plains Drifter* was a weakness of will; and he was totally innocuous in *Bite the Bullet*. Martin has been seen as a mad herpetologist in *Sssssss* and a self-serving hockey team manager in *Slapshot*; and was 99% sympathetic as an ex-con in *Fool's Parade* and as a Depression-era New Orleans junkie in *Hard Times*. These efforts notwithstanding — and certainly not to be ignored in this chapter — the John Wayne films of Donner, and *The Wild Bunch* of Martin and Jones not only contain some of the best heavies from this trio's collective repertoire; but they offer some of the most harrowing villains of all the Old West's film depictions.

Trustworthy? Loyal? Helpful? Robert Donner's response to "Were you ever a Boy Scout?" gives us more cause for disillusionment about the lads in khaki. I opened our interview with that question, and Donner told me, "I was a Tenderfoot for four years, the reason being that the troop to which I belonged was taught to *tie knots*, and once they learned to tie knots, they took the smallest scout they could find—which happened to be myself—*bound* him and *gagged* him with their brand new knots, put him behind the piano, and let him fend for himself. It usually took me at least half to three-quarters of the meeting to set myself free, therefore I learned very little in the scouts, and never progressed beyond the first rank." Donner related this bit of drollery with the skill of a practiced comic, a rich talent he was seldom allowed to sport before a national audience until becoming Exidor, a semi-regular lunatic on the hit television series *Mork and Mindy*, and one of its few guests to rob thunder from Robin Williams, its brilliant comic star. Previously Donner's wit only went out piecemeal in the form of comedy sketches he wrote and performed for charity functions, or anonymously through material he supplied other entertainers, "quite a number of people you'd know," he muttered archly, "who would rather I didn't tell you who they are." Not surprisingly, he is also a veteran of *Your Show of Shows*, once joining Caesar and Coca on a revival tour, and taking over parts originally played by Carl Reiner. Stretching into another comic medium, he fulfills a youthful ambition to be a cartoonist by designing humourous greeting cards for friends.

One other real-life aspect of Robert Donner, running quite contrary to his trigger-happy screen image, came up in our discussion of his hobbies. He confessed to being a sports nut, having always been athletically inclined, and graded himself a "C" tennis player and a seven-handicap golfer. For the cameras he was keeping his meanly lean physique by swimming and general workouts, and said that occasionally he and his wife would go hiking in the Sierras. Hunting, however, was definitely not one of his sports, and he stated adamantly, "I *hate guns*."

At any rate, Robert Donner's tall, sinewy frame is at home against a Western panorama. Although he was born in New York City, his family relocated to New Jersey, to Michigan, and finally to El Paso, Texas, where he graduated from high school. This took place on a Friday with Selective Service ready to grab him the next Wednesday. He sidestepped the Army by enlisting in the Navy on a Monday and served four years, or as he glumly pinpointed, "three years, eleven months, twenty-nine days, and six-and-a-half hours."

Following his discharge from the Navy, Donner earned an associate degree from Valley Junior College in Van Nuys, California, and studied acting for eight years with Jack Kosslyn, a drama coach at Warner Brothers and Universal Studios. He still attends a weekly workshop to keep his "acting muscles" limber between assignments but it was his regimen of physical—rather than professional—fitness that happened to land him his first movie. In 1962 Donner was playing in Hollywood's Entertainers' Softball League for the United Jewish-Italians with such teammates as Don Rickles and Frankie Avalon. Jerry Lewis was sponsoring another team in the league, and at the time he was casting actors as college students for *The Nutty Professor*, Donner was one of several ballplayers who came to Lewis's attention. "For that," Donner affirmed, "I'm forever in Jerry's debt. The job ran for eight weeks, and I was really nothing more than a glorified extra. The one good thing about it was that I learned what everybody did on a set — why you use a certain lens, why you had so much light in one area, not so much in the other — generally how a motion picture was made." Better still, it lined him up for Lewis's next picture, *The Disorderly Orderly*, where Donner met his wife, actress Cissy Wellman.

Because of his varied professional experience on screen, in television, and on stage (the most prestigious medium), Robert Donner can rightly be described as well rounded — but he makes no high-flown claims. He readily admitted a lack of credentials from that footlit Mecca, the New York theater. "No, I've never been on Broadway. The only time I played New York was in an old television show where I played an Indian at Yankee Stadium." Most of the plays he had done were in California, "original works, old chestnuts." But what of the classics? Was not a background in classical theater considered the crowning feather in any actor's cap? Donner countered this attitude with an observation hard to contest. "As far as the classics go ... I have no urge to *do* them! I assume by the classics," he asked me, "that you mean Shakespeare and the like?

"I think the British do a *marvelous* job with Shakespeare — and I think they do a *rotten* job with *O'Neill*! I think *we* do a *good* job with O'Neill, and a *rotten* job with Shakespeare. So, leave them to what they do well, and leave us to what we do well. Shakespeare as an exercise? Fine! But the professional performances I have seen thus far by American companies of Shakespeare — *or* Molière, or *any* of the classic pieces — the language has always gotten in their way. Everybody was so conscious of how they spoke, and exactly what they said, that you were watching *ac*tors *act*. With the English, Shakespeare just does not seem to come over that way."

But again, his stage efforts aside, Donner's television and film heavies have reached the widest audience, and formed his reputation. His features adapt so easily to the weathered, hangdog look of a Western tough or a good-ol'-boy that they have qualified him for a long procession of "character" parts; and while "character actor" is a label some performers shirk, Donner wears it proudly. He lists himself in the "Characters" section of the *Players Directory*. Still, the routine system of casting a Hollywood film make it practical for supporting actors to advertise under "Leading Man" as well. Donner clarified an issue raised in Chapter II, that of dual listings, by offering a rationale for his own. "In many cases producers may be looking in the front of the book for leading men, attempting to cast that part. Well, if they happen to run across my picture there, I'm brought to their mind; and they may think of me in a different way, or for some other part they haven't gotten around to yet. It's just a matter of bringing yourself to the attention of people who can hire you."

"Would you like to play lead roles some day?" I asked.

"Certainly," he replied, adding just as strongly, "but I don't want to quit playing character roles either. And I don't want to stop playing heavies, and I love to play comedy. I don't care *what* kind of work it is, just as long as it's *work*. *I enjoy working*. I'd be very happy to do a new job every *week*!"

"But why so many heavies? Why do you think casting directors have repeatedly put you in that slot?"

"I would assume," he considered, "that when they think of me or choose me, they do so because I have a physical look they feel is right for a character; and I think there is something about the *way* I do it that makes it different ... or at least, I *hope* so."

Discussing his heavies from *El Dorado*, *Chisum* and *Rio Lobo* — all John Wayne Westerns — I caught myself parroting an offhandedness commonly used to describe a body of work that, for Robert Donner, has meant bread and butter. "John Wayne Western" has become almost a generic term, is often used disparagingly, and is generally founded on a disaffection for Wayne himself. While for me the term held no scornful connotations, I hypothesized for Donner a critic's insinuation that he had been acting in second-rate material, mere updates of the old B-Western. What would be his response?

"*El Dorado* was the first time I did work with 'Duke'," Donner stolidly declared, "and I must say that it was a ver-r-r-ry strange experience. I had grown up watching John Wayne on a screen twenty-five feet tall, and when I first saw him in the flesh, I was in *awe*. I've worked with him on five pictures since that time, and I'm *still* in awe of 'im! I think he's a *hell* of an actor because — when you look back on his career — he's been saying roughly the *same damn thing* over and over again, and he *still* makes it sound like it's the first time he's *said* it! And I also think that the toughest thing to do is to play yourself, and to play someone bigger than life as he does. I think he's a *helluva* guy!"

"Up to that time, *El Dorado* was your biggest film," I said, "then *Cool Hand Luke* came close behind it. These were pretty good boosts for you, weren't they?"

"I would say they were both breaks for me, because they were class pictures. *El Dorado* had John Wayne, Bob Mitchum and Jimmy Caan; *Cool Hand Luke* was with Paul Newman. And there is something about riding with a winner. They did good business, they were well received, and as a result when you would go for an interview and the casting director or producer or somebody says, 'Well, what have you been doing lately?'; when you mention *El Dorado* or *Cool Hand Luke*, they may not actually remember *you* from the picture, but they remember the picture was well received, and a positive thing. So in that way, they were considerable breaks."

"For some reason, *Cool Hand Luke* never seems to diminish in power. The oppressiveness of the prison conditions, the brutality of the 'bosses' — yours included — the malfeasance of the 'Cap'n,' and the total control they all had over the inmates' lives come across more convincingly there than practically any other prison movie. Likewise, it's stunning to watch so many actors in *Luke* who've become important since that time: George Kennedy, Strother Martin, Ralph Waite, Anthony Zerbe, Joe Don Baker, J.D. Cannon — nearly every person in the film is now either a star or much in demand as a supporting player. What was it about *Cool Hand Luke* that gave it such emotional force, that made it so special?"

"The one thing I remember," Donner said, "was it was the only time I've ever been on a picture where we had a week's rehearsal. The company came up to Stockton, California, and for two to three hours a day we'd go off on the road, prisoners in their uniforms, and the guards in their uniforms. The guards would stand with their guns and the prisoners would just start hackin' away at the side of the road ... and as the week progressed, an invisible division began to occur. It wasn't anything we were working at, it was just ... the prisoners kinda stayed to themselves, and the guards stayed to *them*-selves ... and the *boredom* of it all began to hang in, and the *guns* just became a *weight* on you. This just evolved naturally, and I think that it comes across in the film. It wasn't anything you had to be conscious of in the morning when you arrived for work. We all came out on the same bus; but as we went and dressed, as we put on the costume, as we started to move around ... you may have ridden out with a guy who was playing a prisoner and just had a great conversation, talked everything over, had breakfast with him. All of a sudden, when you get out there and start putting on the wardrobe ... he just kind of e-e-eases away and starts talking to the other guys who are playing prisoners. And *you* just kind of move toward the other guards."

"While you were working on the film, could you foresee the impact this project ultimately had, as well as its having a 'graduating senior play' quality for so many of your fellow workers?"

"I did feel that we were making something special, something a little bit better. Conrad Hall, who was the cinematographer on the film, was *extremely* enthusiastic. He'd say, 'Let's dig a hole and put the camera down in here!' 'Let's climb a tree and put the camera up there!' Let's do this, let's do that ... a tremendous *enthusiasm*, and everybody was caught up in it. And it *was* an extremely well cast picture. Everybody has just done marvelously since that film, and at the time the only one you really knew very much about was Newman. *He* was the only *star*, but a lot of stars have come *out* of that film!"

Robert Donner 111

"Were you pleased with it — not just the experience, but with the final product?"

"I must say," Donner remarked, "that it takes me about five years before I forget all the little things that were going on, the little things that were happening — 'Oh, this was the day it rained ... that's the day that the set fell down ... that's the day that the kid got hit by the car' — so that you can't look at the scene as an *audience*. The suspense is out of it for you because you've read the script. You know what's going to happen at the end. I find that it takes about five years before you forget all that crap and you can just go in there and *look* at it."

Aside from the dismal aspects of his character and the subject matter of *Cool Hand Luke*, plus calamities that hit the set, Donner assured me there were lighter moments, too. He shared one with me about a key scene in the film, recalling, "Strother Martin and I were rehearsing by the pool at the Stockton Inn the day before we did the scene where Luke is brought back and he's now going to be chained; the world-famous scene of 'What we have here is a failure to communicate.' Well, I was playing Luke, and Strother and I are in our bathing suits, and Strother has twisted up a towel. He is now rehearsing his scene, saying, 'What we have here is a *failure* to *communicate*,' and Luke is spitting or whatever he does, and all of a sudden Strother starts telling me" (breaking into a nasal tenor imitative of Martin) "'Don' yew *nev*-uh tawk tuh me lak that, yew he-uh? Yew *he-uh*?!' And he starts rappin' the crap outta me with this towel.

"Well, there are two little old ladies sitting across the pool, and *we* hadn't paid any attention to *them*. *We're* havin' a *good* time. They took one look at all this, and they jump up screamin' and go running for the desk.

"All I could hear all night long was Strother with this, 'Don' yew nevuh tawk tuh me lak that ag'in, *yew he-uh*?!' Strother always talks like he just got hit in the chest with a two-by-four. Anyway, the next day — now we're doin' it for *real* — once I have put the chains on Luke, I have to stand there and listen to Strother do this thing, and *now* it is striking me *funny*! Well, I am just standing there lock-jawed, looking straight ahead and trying to think of everything under the sun from Ted Williams's batting average to how many consecutive games Joe DiMaggio hit in, anything to keep my mind off what Strother is saying to Luke."

Coincidentally this brought to mind another circumstance requiring from Donner a supreme effort to hold composition, one he added to further illustrate this unusual test of an actor's skills. In *Agent from H.A.R.M.* he portrayed a morgue attendant, aptly long-faced, now and then exhibiting victims of a lethal substance that turned their cadavers into masses of red fungus. "*H.A.R.M.* was an independent picture made out of a car lot in North Hollywood. I always remember it because the bodies — supposedly shot with a 'spore gun' — were made of Jello with little cherries for their eyes. Every time we had to open up the cabinet to bring the body out for viewing, we just had to *steel* ourselves from breaking up, because we knew, 'Here comes the Jello Man again!"

As long as we were in the territory of whimsy, I asked Donner about his deft comic portrayal of Angel Moon in 1972's *something big*. A violent Western it was, Moon along with it, but Donner was a persistent source of laughter. Moon, on sight, was instantly frightful and funny. Dirty-faced, crowned with a dingy bowler, his tight-lipped scowl could as easily belong to a pouting little boy. Even as a killer his villainy resulted in humor, albeit very black humor.

Donner takes little credit for the sharply defined character he rendered, citing screenwriter James Lee Barrett instead. "One hell of a writer," he declared. "Jimmy Barrett is the only guy I know who, when he puts it down on paper, you don't have to rewrite it, you don't have to change it around at all. The words just come right off your tongue. Angel Moon was a character that he created on paper, and *I* just read the *script*." The uncommon twist Barrett gave to Moon was plainest in a scene involving Donner and actors Albert Salmi and David Huddleston. In the plot of *something big* Donner played sidekick to Salmi, a procurer of hard-to-get items. They had agreed to furnish a Gatling gun to Dean Martin and his gang who, in turn, planned to use it in looting treasure from a Mexican bandit stronghold. Salmi's supplier was a paunchy smuggler, played by Huddleston. At the rendezvous point, Huddleston sat gorging himself while calmly holding firm to a price much higher than one prearranged. As Salmi bickered and Huddleston stuffed more food into his own mouth, Salmi felt the whir of sharp steel sail past his ear. A knife sank deep into the chest of the smuggler, whose mouth dropped open, dribbling coffee and masticated food down his chin. The deadpan Angel Moon leaned forward in his saddle, stared hatefully at Huddleston from under the soiled derby that shaded his leathery face, and muttered, "He ate like a pig" — which has to be the flimsiest excuse for killing a man to ever go down on film.

Near the end of *something big*, Moon lost his temper and, for the rash action of drawing against Dean Martin, paid with his life. The esteem his fellow desperadoes held for Moon was expressed by Salmi. Martin asked Salmi if he wanted to bury his friend. "Naah," he sighed. "Maybe something'll come down outta the mountains tonight and drag 'im off."

I poised for a moment on the next question, not quite certain how to phrase it. "I'm not taking anything away from you when I say this," I began, "because I think you've done a super job in your career as far as the work that I've seen; but you'll have to admit that most of your roles — Moon is exceptional on both counts — but most of your roles not only have a low profile, they're also usually very short-lived. Is it worth it, all the training you've undergone just to walk in front of a camera for only a small fraction of the film and often to be killed off?"

During the half-minute the phone line was quiet, Donner formulated as concise a philosophy of playing the heavy that anyone could ask for. "I think what applies here is, 'The end justifies the means'," he responded. "If you recall, in *Chisum* I was riding on my horse with my red long johns on, just having been yanked out of a cathouse. I had my arms tied and Billy the Kid comes along and shoots me out of the saddle. *Hell* of an ending.

"In *El Dorado* I try and get Duke to go out the door into an ambush, he won't go out the door, he says *I* go out the door, I say '*Please* don't do that to me,' he punches the hell of out me, then I go out the door and my *friends* shoot me.

"In *Rio Lobo* my character Whitey wasn't around very long, but he comes in all smart 'n' sassy and the *girl* blows his brains out.

"The *end* justifies the *means*. If you see the film, you've *got* to be aware that the characters I played were *there*; and *that*, I think, is the reason you do it. It's a piece. It's a small piece of the overall picture, but when it's over I think that you *remember* those characters.

"My feeling about heavies is ... there's no such thing, really, as a 'heavy.' They're misunderstoods. Whenever I play a heavy, a character who is misunderstood, I try to justify why this man is doing what he's doing. If I can believe in *my* own mind that what I'm doing is *right*, I think it makes the character more believable. Heavies are not just heavies to be heavies. A man doesn't *just* kick a dog or hit another human being or shoot someone. He does it for some *reason*. If an actor is doing a good job, every heavy honestly believes that what he is doing is *right*.

"Angel Moon was a misunderstood. He didn't like *anybody*. He didn't like any-*thing*. Now in your own mind, you try to *justify* why he feels that way. Why is he hanging in with Albert Salmi? Salmi is a means to an end for Moon, but if Salmi turned on him, Moon would kill *him too*!

"Moon doesn't say much, and doesn't like anybody; and he's *fun* to play, because you just stand there, look at people, and say over and over in your mind" (reverting to Moon's pinch-mouthed drawl), "'Yew ain't worth shee-it.' If anything's going for you, that attitude comes out in your face.

"Also, those characters are fun to play because the audience is just waiting for that moment when he *gets* it. It's simple retribution! Moon is a rotten guy, but Moon will *get* it," he intoned bodefully, "before the picture is over. They *want* 'im to get it, and eventually they're *satisfied*.

"Speaking of 'getting it'," Donner added, "when we did *something big*, we were down in Durango, Mexico; and the director, Andy McGlaglen, was having ... not a good day. It was a *rotten* day, the wind was blowing and it was dirty and miserable and one thing and the other. I was the last shot of the day and he said" (assuming an officious tone), "'All right Donner, now *get* over there and *lay* down. Now, you're *dead*, so *don't breathe*! Uh ... get your *arm* up the way you had it when you got shot ... okay. Open your mouth up! You had your *mouth* open, you know. Open ... all right. Okay, now don't breathe.'" Donner addressed a phantom cameraman. "'All right, roll. Action.'

"I'm there with my mouth open, not breathing. The dust is blowing, and finally—I don't know how long it was—I choked on the *dirt* in my *mouth*, and I coughed and came up.

"When I came up and looked around, there was not a soul left on the set. All the lights were out, the cameras were gone, the people were gone, and the only one there out by the dressing room was my driver. So, I went and got in my car, went back to the motel, got into the shower, and the phone rang. I came out, answered the phone, said, 'Hello' and this voice—it was McGlaglen—said, 'Cut it.' Nice guy, no?"

I could almost see him smirking on the other end, and wondered aloud what the chances were for the public to see even more of the lighter side of Robert Donner.

"I think that one day I'll get an opportunity to do more comedy," he said, "and I hope that I'll be able to do both: play the heavies and character roles, and also play comedic roles. It would be the best of all possible worlds. Ed Asner is a great example of that. When Ed was getting started, all he got was heavy roles, heavies, heavies. Then along came *The Mary Tyler Moore Show* and everybody said, 'My God, he can do *comedy*,' like it was a big surprise. *He's a fine actor*!"

"In either the lead or the supporting field of actors," I posed, "whom do you personally admire? Is there anyone you've ever tried to emulate?"

"I think one of the finest heavies ever was Robert Ryan, who was in person an extremely liberal man. His performance in *Billy Budd*, I think, is one of the most chilling heavies there *ever* was. Another actor I've always admired is Brian Keith. I just enjoy watching him work. I enjoy seeing anything Strother does—Strother Martin is just a fine actor. I can't say that I ever tried to 'emulate' anyone. I admired Paul Muni immensely. John Carradine I've always enjoyed in whatever he did. Van Heflin was fine... Thomas Mitchell... I've just always been enamored of character actors and character actresses. They were always old friends that I was glad to see again."

"Whenever a movie is reviewed," I noted, "it seems most often the critic spends his time talking about the stars, and gives short shrift to supporting actors in the film, even if they did an excellent job. Do you think current supporting actors and character actors should be given more attention for what they do?"

"There *should* be more attention paid to supporting players, yes!" Donner asserted. "In the old days of Hollywood, the studios realized the value of good support. When they had a new actor they wanted to groom for stardom, they put him in and *protected* him with good, solid people. I don't think the critics today, *or* the studios, know how much the general public enjoys seeing character actors, and what they mean."

"Has the lack of fanfare around your own career left you fairly anonymous to the general public?"

"I'm recognized occasionally. I was in Oklahoma recently, and saw a lady coming right at me, and I *knew* she was coming to *me*. She had this big smile on her face, and when she got over to me she said, 'I'm sorry, I don't know what your name is, but I *know* I don't *like* you.' In most cases people are very surprised to find out that you're a halfway decent human being. They *are* a bit *reticent* to strike up a conversation with you right off the bat, because there *is* that ... that separation they feel. They really don't know what kind of reaction they're going to get from you because of the type of parts that you do play."

"Do you have a favorite role, or something you consider your best work to date?"

"I couldn't really say what's my best piece of work. That's up to someone else. That's up to an audience to tell *me* what they think is my best piece of work, which part they were particularly affected or moved by. In the end, that's who dictates it all.

"I'd say my favorite role is the *next* role. What I've done in the past, under the given circumstances I did the best job that I could. This is not to say I couldn't do it better in five years, because I'd have five more years to observe human nature, five more years of laughter, tears, fear. I'd just be a better instrument in five years, so maybe I could do a *better* job *then*; but at the given time, I did the best job that I could."

"What about money? Do you feel like you've been fairly rewarded for your services?"

"I don't know whether I'm adequately compensated for my work or not," Donner replied, not guardedly as if personal finances were too private a matter, but more in bemusement, as if his normal preoccupations seldom included them. "All I can say is that the only time that I am *really happy* is when my ass is in canvas, and I'm sitting on a set. When I die, I'd like to *die* on a *set*. I *love* actors, I *love* to be around them, and I *love* to be working; and I'm always pleasantly surprised when a check arrives. They've *paid* me for doing what I *love to do*!"

"Then there are more reasons than money to keep you hanging in there?"

"I've met some marvelous people," he said. "I have some tremendous, extremely talented friends and, as a result of being an actor, I am asked to go all over the world and meet so many different people. So many people," he expressed in bewilderment, "are born and die within a one hundred mile radius. They never get a chance to get out, meet other people, find out what *they're* thinking of, what *their* worries and joys are. I have a nice home, a wonderful wife, I get to travel, I work at a job that I love. I consider it a twenty-four-hour-a-day job, because you're constantly observing your fellow man, and you never know when you're gonna be called on to play that type of part that you've just spotted in the flesh.

"You have to remember one thing about acting," Donner said, "and that is that your last job may be your *last job*. There's *nothing* to say you're gonna *work* again. Conceivably, you could *never* work *again!* You've run through every debt, every favor, every friend, and now it's all over. They've finally caught up to you!

"I'm not looking for financial security as an actor. I think it's ridiculous to do so. If it comes, that's fine. My wife and I live well, we enjoy it, and it's all been brought about as a result of my being an actor—but it could all end tomorrow. And if it ends tomorrow, fine! If I have to dig ditches, I'll *dig* ditches... But I can *still perform*. I can perform for *nothing!* They can't take *that* away from me. Whatever it is that they hire Robert Donner for may go out of style, and if it does go out of style, then I'll find something else to do, and it's been *great!* I'm a much better human being for every moment that I've put into being an actor, and I've gotten more out of it than I've ever put in." [April 1976.]

Notwithstanding his long string of heavies, I hadn't "heard a discouraging word" from Robert Donner; and judging by L.Q. Jones's buoyancy as we discussed his own career, for him "the skies are not cloudy all day." He threw himself into an interview with the alacrity of an accomplished storyteller. The accents of his native Texas shaped the words rolling off his tongue, and as Jones showed no impatience to get a question answered and out of his way, it was obvious he was guided by a back porch passion from home, a relish for settling down and hashing everything over.

I phoned Jones on a busy afternoon at the office of his modestly successful film production company, L.Q. Jones and Friends. Unavoidably, we were interrupted several times during the interview. It was something he predicted would happen, but he fielded each inquiry from his secretary with good humor and disposed of it with a comment, or a noisily dashed off memo to himself. Overhearing this bustle brought to mind the energy that permeates his film and television characters; namely that, whatever their objective, they seem to attack it with boyish glee. There was his gabby Marine recruit in *Battle Cry* and an Army counterpart in *The Naked and the Dead*. There was his lynch law vigilante in *Hang 'em High*; T.C., his raffish, moronic posse rider in *The Wild Bunch*; the thieving, raping fur trapper of *Winterhawk*; or Black Harris, a wily, smooth-talking ally of William Bonnie in *Pat Garrett & Billy the Kid*. Ever fitting in these modes were Jones's vulpine looks—a thatch of dingy yellow hair, thick mustache, and a feral smile lurking just beneath the surface if it ever disappeared at all—looks that would be equally at home on a sheep country bounty poster. Regarding them when asked to compose a résumé describing himself, he was not above self-deprecation. "I am six-feet," he responded, "I weigh one-seventy-five, my eyes are somewhat..." (crooning) "mi-i-isty blu-u-ue ... ('rheumy' I guess is the word). My hair has been dyed so many different colors in the last five years, I don't know what color to say. Kind of straw blond." Playing it straight, he added for the record, "I was in the Navy. Formal education at the University of Texas in Austin, Lon Morris Junior College in Jacksonville, Lamar State College of Technology in Beaumont. I am but several hours away from three degrees: one in law, one in business, and one in journalism."

"'L.Q.' has a nice Western ring to it. Is this why you keep your name in initial form?" I asked.

"No," Jones chuckled. "It is the name the studio gave me after I did a role in the picture *Battle Cry*, and it was the name of my character, 'L.Q. Jones.' That seemed to be rather in vogue at that time, so I said, 'What the heck!' They wanted me to change it and I didn't care, so long as they made the checks out properly. It's the name I'm used to now, and everybody knows me by it."

"Since you're apparently not the illiterate vulgarian you generally portray, I was wondering. What kind of reading material do you like? What kind of music?"

"I'm hodgepodge and oatmeal, I guess. I like everything. I don't find myself categorized one way or the other," Jones said. "I like comic books; I like the classics. I like the Beatles; I like opera. As long as it is good, the name you hang onto it is very unimportant to me. I like someone to do a good job, whatever he's doing."

"I guess your being from Texas is what makes the accents usually called for in your characters, Southern and Southwestern, sound so authentic," I said.

"Southern accent is fairly easy to come up with. Southwest is very tough because it is not really an accent, but a *manner* of speaking. For some reason, we push most of the sound up into the top of our mouth and use our nose a great deal. Other people trying to imitate that have a heck of a time because it is a *way* of speaking, I guess, and you learn it over the years and it is very hard to do automatically. Hence, you will find very few people that do use it properly.

"I can switch around, as far as accents are concerned. Like many people who did come from the South, of course — and I did come from the Southwest, being Texas — we try to *lose* part of the accent because it makes it very difficult in this business if you can *only* work with an accent. I've worked at it a little bit. I still stick with it some. I would like to lose possibly a little bit more ... and yet I guess I'm pretty much me. I'm going to speak the way I speak, so I'll stick with that."

"Most of your pictures are action-packed, with lots of gun-play and galloping. Was there something in your early days that prepared you for all this rough-and-tumble?"

"I did a little hunting," Jones replied. "I was raised, had been around horses ... not that much. We had them available for the weekends, and I rode a bit. Mainly I was very heavy into competitive sports, played a little professional baseball, played football until I had the legs broken. I like sports of all kinds, participate in most. I'm not much of an onlooker. I like to get involved in it."

"Do you still keep some kind of diet or exercise program now to stay in shape?"

"No," he answered wryly, "when you're 'pore,' you tend to stay that way automatically."

"Okay!" I announced, marking an end of preliminaries and cueing him for the standard opener: "How did it all start? How did you get in the movies?"

"Ya wanna know how I got started?" Jones's voice had a lilt, re-enacting the scene between the self-made tycoon and the cub reporter. "All right." He wound himself up with a deep breath, harumped, and commenced his yarn. "Here goes. My very first picture was *Battle Cry*, which we did in 1954–55. Fess Parker and I were roommates in college. He had come out to Hollywood and just started—he had not yet done Davy Crockett. I was ranching at the time in Nicaragua, and he sent me a copy of the book *Battle Cry* saying that he thought he was going to be in the picture. I read it and said, 'What the heck, I think I'll go play the part of L.Q. Jones!' which was in the book. I arrived in L.A. Fess drew me a map on the back of a shirtboard, and I wheeled out to Warners in all my innocence. It so happened when I got there, they had the old dual entry-and-exit way with one guard.

"Now, if you don't have an appointment, you don't get into the majors to see people; but since I had no appointment, I go sailing up to the gate, and just as I got there, a little blonde with a very tight sweater was just coming out the other side. Of course, the guard looked at *her* and just punched the button and let me in. I sailed by *him*, I went into Hoyt Bower's office.

"Now again, it so happened that Hoyt's secretary was out getting coffee. Her name was Kathy. Kathy's very nice people, but she also is used to the system; and *she'd* throw *King Kong* out if he didn't have an appointment. So, she wasn't there, I sailed right in. Hoyt was on the phone, I just walked in his office, put my feet on the desk, and told him when he got through talking on the phone how lucky he was I was here to play the part. He then threw me out.

"The next day I talked my way back in on the telephone. He threw me out again.

"Next day, I talked my way back in again. He said, 'What the heck! Come on, I'll let you talk to Solly Biano.' Solly was head of casting at that time at Warner Brothers. I went to see Solly, Solly spent twenty minutes, thirty minutes telling me why I could not *possibly* be in the picture. He was preparing to throw me out, and about that time the phone rang, and it was Raoul Walsh who was going to direct *Battle Cry*. Somehow or the other the conversation got around to me, and Raoul said, 'I'll tell you what. You send him up, and *I'll* throw 'im out!' So we went up to see Raoul, and when I walked in, there he sat with that patch on his eye sitting behind the desk glowering at me. So I just glowered *back* at him and we just stood and *stared* at each other for about five minutes. Finally he said, 'Ah ... how tall are ya, kid?' I remembered in the book that L.Q. was about five-seven, five-eight. Even though I'm six-feet, I said, 'Oh, I'm about five-seven, five-eight.' He says, 'You're a goddamned liar! Can you learn lots of words?' and I says, '*Oh*, can *I* learn lots of *words!*' and he says, 'Give him a test,' and he threw me out.

"Next day I came over, took the test, they looked at it and they told Walsh, 'Hey, we liked the test. *But*, we've already tested 250 people for that part, all professionals. You're gonna be 6,000 miles away, Raoul. You need somebody you know you can rely on. So, while the test was good, we better go with somebody else.' And for no explicable reason Raoul said, 'I'll tell you what. Either the kid does the part, or you can get yourself another director!' Well! They weren't *about* to lose *Raoul Walsh*, so they said, 'What the heck?' They signed me up to a weak contract telling me of course that when I could not cut it, they would send me back and get somebody else in my stead. But when we got over there, Raoul not only kept the part going, but took parts away from two other actors and gave them to me — which made me very popular with the cast — and we shot the picture for sixteen weeks. And luckily enough, I've been rolling ever since."

"During the intervening years, some of that rolling has been under the direction of Sam Peckinpah. You've had quite a long association with him, haven't you?"

"With Sam I did *Ride the High Country*, then we did *Major Dundee*, then we did the ill-fated *Cincinnati Kid* on which he was fired and I quit, then we did *The Wild Bunch, Cable Hogue, Pat Garrett & Billy the Kid*, one that very few people knew about was *Noon Wine*, and *The Lady Is My Wife*. I was probably Sam's best friend for, I don't know, three or four years; and he was going to direct a picture for me that I was going to produce, and the attorneys stole the money, which kind of put a damper on things for a little while until we got it back, and by that time Sam was busy on one thing and I was busy on another, so we did not do that one."

"In light of the fact that you've been a film director yourself, what do you think of Peckinpah as one, or — shall we say — as an artist?"

"About Peckinpah...," Jones pondered. "As an artist, there are very few people who are his peer. Incidentally, I think he's a better writer than he is a director, and I think he's a *fantastic* director ... or was. I don't much like the stuff he has done recently. Not too many people do, I guess. But Sam's having a tough time right now. He's over in Yugoslavia making a war picture called *Cross of Iron*, so he can kill all the people he wants to, I guess.

"As a director, he is superb. I've picked up a bit of the things Sam does, as far as my being a director. I'm not putting myself in his class by any stretch of the imagination. I'm just saying that I've learned a lot of things from him. His absolute attention and dedication to details is one thing I've learned. That's why a picture like *A Boy and His Dog* — like it or dislike it — you will find the detail of it so infinitely well done that a lot of times you can get by with things that are really wild, if you are very careful in the detail and in the way they are prepared; because, subliminally, the mind will tell you that things are right, that they are going the way they should, and you will just automatically accept them. Without that attention to detail, something will be bothering you about what you are seeing. You will not know *what*, but *something* will bother you, and will take part of your enjoyment away from the picture.

"Sam is excellent in seeing that all of his detail is proper to the extent that — I think it was on *The Wild Bunch* — Sam fired a prop-man because he had not counted the beans on my plate from one shooting to another. We did the master shot first, and then some several weeks later we did close-ups. In the close-ups I had seven beans on my plate, and in the master shot I had thirteen (according to Sam's count). Therefore, the man was fired; which didn't make his case very unusual, because Sam fired ... oh, I don't know ... sixty to sixty-five percent of the crew on *The Wild Bunch* at one time or another. Not all of them left, but they were hired and then fired and then hired again. On *Cable Hogue* we kept a bus that did nothing but run back and forth to the hotel and to the airport, seeing that they could come and go as Sam fired 'em and hired 'em."

"I've interviewed Strother Martin," I told Jones, "and it seems your association with Sam Peckinpah has thrown you two together quite a few times, hasn't it? Do you have any good stories to tell?"

"Aw, Strother and I go back a *number* of years," Jones said. "As a matter of fact, let's see ... the third picture I made was one with Strother called *Target Zero*. We've been friends for a long time. We've worked in Sam's pictures together, we've worked in television together. Stories? I've got *thousands* of them, as anyone does who's worked together with Strother. One time when we did *Cable Hogue*, Strother and I had finished the first part of what we had to do, went back and did some more work, and then Sam got through with us. I went off on another picture, Strother came back here, then towards the last of making *Cable Hogue* Sam got a hair up his nose and decided he just had to have us back. We went back, in a great hurry. He sent a plane for me, cancelled another show I was doing — at least my shooting in it for that day — flew me back, had the limousine at the airport with all the wardrobe and the makeup people in it. I changed on the way, and we jumped out of the car, Strother and I did the shot ... and Strother screwed up.

"Sam jumped *all* over Strother, said, 'You dimwit, you no good klutz!'...

"And so, we did it again. This time, *I* screwed up. *Oh*, and *did* I screw up! But when we started back, Sam was very quiet, and he knew we had a problem. And he's sayin', 'Strother Martin, you dimwit. You're tryin' to run me out of this business. I'll *kill* you. You'll never again work in a picture as long as you live...' He called him everything in the book. *I* just split off, went around back, got something to drink, came back, and Sam was — five minutes later — still *at* 'im.

"And so, I said, 'Sam, listen, I was...'

"He said, '*Shut* up, L.Q., I'm talking to Strother. Strother Martin, you idiot! You dimwit! You numbskull! You no-talented clod!' He went at 'im for another four or five minutes.

"And I'm sayin', 'But Sam, Sam, I was...'

"He said, '*Shut* up, L.Q., just *stay* out of this,' and went on and on and on, and Strother just stood there takin' it.

"*Finally* I got through to 'im and I said, 'Sam, *I* was the one that made the mistake. *I* was the one that screwed up.'

"'...Uh ... is that right, Strother?'

"'...Uh ... yes, it is, Sam.'

"'Strother Martin! You babbling *idiot!* You mean to tell me you *stood* there...' He went back at 'im for another ten minutes. But that's what Strother was around Sam. He was *petrified* of 'im. And every time something went wrong, whether Strother had *anything* to do with it or not, Sam jumped on his back because poor old Strother is such a good whipping boy."

"In your own opinion," I asked, "what are the prerequisites for a heavy? Physique? A drawl? An ethnic type? How is it that you've been assigned to that category for most of your career?"

"How much is a used car?" Jones asked by way of answer. "Sounds like I'm dodging the question? I'm really not. Look at the wide range and variety of heavies that you will find. Since almost every picture has a heavy in one shape, form or fashion ... oh ... you go from Paul Fix, back to the whining days when he was the one who always stabbed you in the back; you go to Paul Gilfoyle, who was somewhat the same, only a little bit dirtier; Elisha Cook, Jr., Laird Kreegar, Jack Palance, Lee Van Cleef, Lee Marvin, Strother, Warren Oates ... we're all different — completely! And of course, different parts call for different heavies. As for what casting directors are looking for when they hire me, it's hard to say. I have a certain presence. I play *against* that presence a lot of times. I started probably one school of being a heavy that kind of came in vogue, and of course I use it, and Warren Oates used it for a while, Jack Elam did with his own twist ... and that's of a heavy that is not crazy or deranged—although we play those, of course—but rather someone who is a heavy because he *enjoys* being a heavy. He enjoys being a *shit!* Oh, gad, I've done twenty-five, thirty, fifty different types of heavies; a shade here, a shade there... It's really hard to say what they're looking for when they pick me. Basically they are looking for an actor to bring something to the part that will make it come *alive*, that will make it *work*. They hire you for many different reasons ... ah, being cheap (cough) ... being available ... being what they are looking for, they think. Of course, they work a lot from things they have seen you do, or from what they have heard someone else say about what you've done. There are all *sorts* of reasons.

"I know when *I'm* casting, I look for someone who is interested in the part, who will bring more to it than just showing up; who will dig for those things that will give it a roundness, because a lot of times your heavy is not that well presented in the script. Most times, he's too one-sided. So, we look for things to bring to being a heavy: a certain softness; a vulner-ability there that makes him human; a quiet moment when he's a screamer most of the time; a look, the way he dresses; the way he walks into a room. There are *many* things that contribute to why a casting director will choose me over someone else ... or someone *else* over *me*."

"I once read a comment by one of your colleagues in the support-ing actor field," I said, turning to the subject of finances. "It boiled down to a complaint that character actors don't get paid enough. Have you felt under-compensated?"

"I don't find from my own experience that I am underpaid, for what I *do*. One might feel—if he looks at the scale—that he is underpaid when compared with the star or the lead of the piece. But then many times I find myself in that spot of being the star or being the guest lead... Then, I guess everyone would always like to get more money.

"I think that most of our stars are *over*-paid rather than a lot of the character people are being *under*-paid. I don't mean that the stars don't earn their money; because they are only paid the money they get because they are *worth* it. Now if that sounds like a stupid statement, look at it a little closer. They're not going to pay Jack Nicholson or Marlon Brando a million dollars, nor anyone else, if they don't reasonably feel that that man can justify his salary at the box office plus the *other* two or three or four million dollars that go into the project. So it is rather a head count or ticket sales that determines an actor's worth at the box office. Now, it's off-center, it's hard to come up with what is the real answer. But with the taxes being what they are today, most people—when they *are* being paid a million dollars a picture, or thirty, fifty thousand dollars a week—*they* don't get to keep it. The *government* keeps *most* of it! So it would seem to me that there could be a more equitable way of determining a pay scale, for *everybody* in our business; especially with the stars' being tied more to box office performance than to just a flat salary.

L.Q. Jones 123

"The problem is, it is so hard to account for money once the picture has gotten out. I'm not saying the people are thieves. We don't have thieves in our business any more than they have 'em in the insurance business or the banking business. But most of us who are actors do not really understand the intricacies of distributing a picture, and why the vast sums of money that are accounted for at the box office become so small when it comes time to divvy up and say who gets what. Consequently, to protect themselves from what they think is an inequity, actors ask for huge sums of money; and the way things are today, stars can get it... But I'm wandering.

"In my own case, I do not feel that I am undercompensated. Yes, I would like to have more money. I don't think I *deserve* it. I don't think I deserve what I *get*. To me, I am fortunate in that I am doing something I really enjoy. I am contributing something, I guess. I'm being paid *more* than a handsome salary. But like most actors who are really involved in the business—and most of us are, or we wouldn't *be* in the business—I would work for a third, or a tenth of what I normally get if the part is *right*. I am not tied to money as a guide for my performance. I perform exactly the same whether I'm getting five thousand dollars a week or five hundred a week ... or *fifty* a week, for that matter. It doesn't make any difference."

"Then an actor's salary, his box office appeal, and recognition factor are somehow tied together," I said. "What about your own notoriety? Do you find that you're well enough known by the general public, even to the point of having 'name recognition'?"

"Yes, I have that," Jones agreed. "It is such that now almost everywhere I go, people recognize me. In a great number of cases they don't know *why* or *where*. They're not sure whether I deliver the milk, or whether I pump gas down at the corner service station; but it rings a bell somewhere, and it *bothers* them. You can always see every time I walk into a group of people where they are not expecting an actor, it begins to make the rounds; but fairly soon someone will come up with the name.

"I'm in that never-never land at the moment where I'm not a big star, certainly not a beginner, and certainly recognizable; and it is comfortable in one respect, because I can go places and do things that many of the big stars cannot do because people will bother you. (And hey! When they *stop* botherin' ya, you better get out of the business and start lookin' for *another* way to make a living). It is not comfortable sometimes when you want to just go somewhere and be part of a crowd and enjoy what you're doing, rather than being somebody *different* from everybody else. But that's part-and-parcel of being in the business, and you better learn to carry it. Almost all people do. All *big* people learn to carry it without too much trouble."

"What about hostile reactions?"

"I hardly ever get those. Oh, somebody in a bar every now and then — which I frequent very seldom — will say, 'Oh, yeah! That *tough guy!* Let's see if you're really as tough as you seem to be in pictures.' You'll find yourself in those sorts of things, but basically people recognize who I am, and they realize it's a job like anything else. But since we actors share their home with them via the television set so many times during the week," he said, a little subdued, "we become sort of neighbors; and people will come up and show me pictures of their children, or of their hunting lodge, or of a fish they caught two years ago; or tell me their problems ... because they consider I'm a friend, and part of the family. It's a very strange feeling, sometimes."

My being less aware of Jones's television ventures as opposed to his films, the latter comment led me to mention that I had spotted him not long before in the space of a week not once, but twice in daily televised reruns of *The Big Valley* — in one, as an especially scroungy villain, he delivered a roundhouse punch to actress Barbara Stanwyck — and that frequence had caused me to wonder if this was just an odd coincidence, or if the deck was stacked in his favor.

"In television I've done about 450 shows," he confirmed, "so, yes, I do a lot of them. *Big Valley*, I did twenty, thirty of them; so, if you watch it over a span of time, I'll probably be on every third or fourth show. I liked to do them because they were just good, basic Westerns and a lot of fun — and Barbara Stanwyck is one of the great troupers of *all* time."

"Between television and film, do you have any preference?"

"Like almost any actor, I would rather work in film, as opposed to television, because television is a hurry-up medium. It is very difficult for writers to write, producers to do their work, directors to do their preparation, crews to get ready to shoot, edit, do all the things that *have* to be done in that short period of time and still have the quality that is necessary for good entertainment. They have a time slot they have to fill every week, therefore they must press on with their schedule. It is fun and creative to work in that atmosphere, but given my choice of the two, I would take film where the added time, to me, is well used ... *could* be well used, and normally lends itself to a better product. That's not necessarily true all of the time, but it has the best chance. The odds are there."

"Would you like to direct for television?"

"We've talked about it a little bit. I am not particularly interested. I'm not even sure I want to direct for anyone else, period, because I direct in a strange way. There are certain things I'm looking for, and I don't get in a hurry if I don't think something is right; and *that* is tough on a *budget* sometimes. So for the moment, at least, I will stick with directing my own projects."

"Before we get to your directorial project of *A Boy and His Dog*, let me ask you something about *The Wild Bunch*," I said. "Your and Strother Martin's characterizations of T.C. and Coffer were superb; and yet, from the reviews I could locate of the film, I couldn't find a single mention of either of you. Why do you suppose this happened?"

"Our business, of course is tied to the big name stars and—neither right nor wrong—that's just the way it is," Jones stated flatly. "*Everybody* would like to change it a *little* bit, I guess, *including* the big name stars. Reviews and reviewers can only do so much in any given time. They only have so much space, therefore they tend like many people to talk about the stars—good, bad, or indifferent—and ignore the *other* people. But like everybody that does work in the character field, it's not necessarily that you *like* it, but you just kind of get *used* to it. In a way, it's sort of a left-handed compliment. Most of us character people are *expected* to do a good job, and even when you *do* an exceptional job, not much attention is paid to it by the critics. They're busy on something else ... and that's fine."

"Does it even concern you what critics say about you, if anything?"

"You *always* care what *anybody* says, whether you say you do or don't. Everyone would like more recognition when he's right, and far less recognition when he's wrong. Invariably, over the past two or three years, when there is a review concerning a picture I am in, I'm almost always mentioned. Why that is, I don't know. Maybe I'm bumping into people who are friends or who have formed an affinity for the work I do."

"After any certain role, have you ever felt that you may have warranted, say, a Best Supporting Actor nomination?"

"Never," Jones answered. "I doubt very seriously if any actor does. It's always rather a surprise when you do."

"Would you have any qualms about accepting an Oscar?"

"If I did the job I thought was worthy of it in the long run, I would be tickled to death to; because it is recognition by your peers, and all of us look for that."

Because of *A Boy and His Dog*, Jones may count among his peers not only actors, but directors and screenwriters. As an independent producer he adapted the futuristic shocker from a Harlan Ellison story, spinning a tale more bizarre than the nightmares of Huxley and Orwell. Like many of Jones's heavies, the film was earmarked by bold outlandishness. Set at a time following global nuclear exchange, life in the American Southwest had reverted to tribalism, to nomadic scavenging of foodstuffs among the ruins. Young men armed with guns, either in bands or singly, took food and women by force as equivalent objects of plunder. In contrast with harsh life on the surface, a subterranean Middle America survived in all its plenty—and all its repressiveness. Jason Robards, Jr., portraying its leader, pontificated from an astro-turfed knoll, seated more as if in a turn-of-the-century parlor and reading death sentences to nonconformists under the light of a Tiffany lamp. Meanwhile, the synthesized diet, artificial lighting, and rigid social structure had caused young males to go sterile.

A nubile young woman, well presented by Susanne Benton, was sent to the surface to retrieve a virile seed bull for a new generation. She chose a youth played by Don Johnson, one of the loners, who kept company with a shaggy, short-legged mutt that conversed with him telepathically, and could locate stores of food and catch the scent of female flesh on the wind; all this in exchange for meals and Johnson's friendship. Not until Johnson was bound and attached to a milking apparatus, denying him the privilege of personally inseminating scores of eligible subterranean girls, did he rebel. He escaped to the surface with Benton only to find that his dog had waited faithfully for days at his point-of-entry to the underground, and was near death from starvation. The girl—off camera, thankfully—became meat for the dog's revival, and launched a trek with his master to a fabled land beyond the mountains.

"The fact that you produced and directed your own picture," I said, "leads me to believe you've achieved a certain amount of respect and leverage in Hollywood. What's the story behind the making of *A Boy and His Dog*? How difficult was it to get the backing and bring the production to the screen?"

"Phew!" Jones reacted. "It would take me five hours to answer that. The story behind it would take an hour or so in itself.

"It *was* difficult. It is difficult to make *any* picture. Once you have been around a motion picture—either in a major field or an independent field—you wonder how one ever gets made, how it ever gets finished, and then how it ever gets on the screen. They are *unbelievably* difficult to do. There are so many things that have to be done, so many things that have to be done right. *A Boy and His Dog* was a shade more difficult, I guess, than most. We had the leverage, of course, because it was our fourth picture. Each one has made money, so we have that as our selling point, and the ability to raise money goes with it—although most of the money in this particular picture was mine and Alvy Moore's, money that we had pyramided from the other pictures."

"How did *A Boy and His Dog* do financially?" I asked.

"A picture always falls short of what you anticipate in your earnings, because you would of course like it to be *Jaws* (*ahem*). It was not. It has done a very healthy business, a very good business. I would guess that our picture has grossed to date an amount of money that puts it in the top fifteen percent of all pictures made and released in seventy-five–seventy-six."

"What about the critical response?"

"We are very gratified with it, because ours is a very strange, a very unusual picture; and when you do something very strange and unusual, a lot of times the critics will come down heavy on your back. When you try something different, you're of course in a new field, and the tendency is to make mistakes. We made our share of mistakes, but in most parts the critics were very kind to us. I have in my files maybe 150 reviews. Twenty-five of them say things like, 'It is the best science fiction movie ever made' — 'Certainly in the Top Five science fiction pictures ever made' — 'A gem!' — 'Fantastic!' Of the remaining 125, 100 of them, 115 let's say, would say, 'It is a good picture' — 'It is an excellent picture' — 'It's charming' — 'It's funny' — 'It's grotesque' — 'It's brutal' — 'I like this ... I like that' — 'That was superb ... this was not good' — 'You may like it. Go see it!' Ten of the 150 say, 'It's the worst piece of garbage ever made' — 'It should be *burned*' — 'I *hated* it' — 'I *detested* it.' And in one respect they are paying something of homage to the picture, because any time a picture can involve you to the point where you get *furious* at what you have seen, then it's done its job properly. You will find very few people who sit on the fence with this picture and say, 'Well, uhmmm ... ahhh ... you know, I'm not sure...' They either love it or hate it. There's very little in between. Full of mistakes, as any motion picture will be. We love it and we're very proud of it, and I would still love to go back and do it all over again."

"It must have been a real privilege to direct Robards," I observed, "recipient of that Best Supporting Actor Oscar we were talking about. Did you have any trouble landing him?"

"No. He read the piece and thought he'd like to do it. All we had to do was work out the money. (That always is a problem.) To me, Jason is the finest technician in our business today, bar none. All you have to do is let him know exactly what you have in mind and then stand back and give him room, because *he* can *do* it."

"I'm sure you've heard the great outcry from actresses for more good roles to play. I think you may have answered that complaint with the female lead of *A Boy and His Dog*. What about other film properties?" I asked. "Are you currently developing any others for directing in the near future?"

"As far as roles for actresses go," Jones assured, "there are not that many of them. As far as roles for *actors* go, there are not that many of them. *Good* parts are hard to come by. A good *property* is *unbelievably* hard to find. We are looking very hard. We have not yet found that thing to which we want to dedicate ourselves for the next year or so, working on; but we're looking, and somewhere along the line it's hidden."

"This is usually considered an unfair question when put to actors," I apologized, "but since you're such a sporting fellow, you get it anyhow. Out of your many co-stars, with whom did you especially enjoy working?"

"I'm not being a Pollyanna about this," Jones offered in a believe-it-or-not tone, "because you will find as I go along I'll pretty well say what I please. I cannot recall working with an actor or an actress when it was *not* enjoyable. Almost everyone approaches his job differently and does it a different way — that's why there are so many of us in the business. Almost everyone responds to someone who works hard. I work hard, and I have a good time. But to me, it would be very difficult to single out any one person, or even two or three or four. I've *thoroughly* enjoyed working with people like Elvis Presley, like Bill Holden, Chuck Heston, Marlon Brando, Montgomery Clift, Barbara Stanwyck. I've thoroughly enjoyed working with Strother Martin, Lee Van Cleef, Warren Oates, Slim Pickens, Ben Johnson, and fifteen or twenty other people in that category. It's hard to single out."

"Getting back to acting, your villains—from T.C. in *The Wild Bunch* to Black Harris in *Pat Garrett & Billy the Kid*, to the trucking boss in *White Line Fever*, to the trapper in *Winterhawk*—all come across so forcefully that they leave an after-image on the brain. How do you make that happen? What's the secret?"

"I don't accredit anything in particular to what I do. I approach each role differently, looking for a different handle in each case, something to be a little bit unusual—because if you are usual," Jones reflected, "then someone else has your job, I guess. Each character has its own nuance. Each character should be done a little bit different, and that I try.

"What works for me, I guess it works for me by *being* that person I am trying to portray. I do not attempt to 'act' as such, as do very few actors. I attempt to *be*. For that moment in time, that is the person I am. When you see me on the screen and I am mad at someone, I am literally *furious* at that person at that given instant. As soon as the camera goes off, then *I* click off. I go back to who I am and what I am. But at that point in time, *that* is the way I am, *that* is the way I feel, *that* is what I am trying to say. I detest that person I don't like; or I love that person, if I'm supposed to do it that way. Bottom-lining, I'm just saying that I *am*, rather than acting-to-be, that person."

"What would you say has been your finest hour, your best piece of work?"

"Gad! I've had so many of 'em, it would be just impossible to list here ... and as a matter of fact, I hope my finest hour hasn't *been* yet.

"My best piece of work ... oh, gad! As I say, I've done fifty some-odd pictures and 450 television shows. Of course, some will be more favored, like *The Wild Bunch*. I had a great deal of fun doing that, but it's not my favorite because I don't *have* a favorite. If I were really just pinned down and had to say something, I would guess the character I did on *Cimarron Strip* called Lummy would be my favorite. That was one featuring Joseph Cotten and Stu Whitman, of course. There were so many sides to Lummy. There were so many things to do. He was such a character in and to himself, and it was one of those things that comes along quite literally once every five or ten years, and I just happened to be fortunate enough to do it. I have never seen anything quite like him before or since. If you did not see it, it was a character who *was* a heavy—a whiner at times, brutal at times, funny at times—but he was quite literally two different characters. I even used two different voices for him in that he talked to himself. Now, that's very difficult to do and not have it come off like the old prospector talking to his jackass; but in that particular case it worked, and so it was a great deal of fun.

"But again I would have to say, what I did in *Battle Cry*, what I did in *White Line Fever*, what I've done in the *Gunsmokes* and *The Virginians*, *The Young Lions* ... gad! There's just no end to it.

"I enjoy working, I enjoy people I'm around, it is *fun* to be creative and it's fun to hope that somewhere along the line you *entertain* people." [July 1976.]

If it takes the best to back the best, Strother Martin stands at the head of his league. The consummate character actor shared the screen with some of Hollywood's biggest stars, and in recent years before his death he attained a respectable position in the credits for himself as well. He appeared with such leading men as James Coburn, Charles Bronson, and Robert Redford, and repeatedly with John Wayne, James Stewart, Paul Newman, and Lee Marvin; but never, it seemed, did such luminaries outshine him.

Strother Martin is probably best known for a succession of rednecks and scruffy Western tramps, especially for the brutal Cap'n of *Cool Hand Luke* and the truly gritty Coffer of *The Wild Bunch*. It was his gift, however, to endow many of his frauds, losers, undesirables and scapegraces with a quality that borders on the endearing. Martin was not an imposing man. In our telephone interview he recounted to me a wardrobe fitting for a certain film, during which he was asked his height. "Five-eight," he replied, "and that's stretchin' the hell out of it." He described his walk as looking "like a bad imitation of Bob Hope," and his voice as sounding "like Shirley Temple with a cold"; and yet, these made for a bantam pugnacity, a world-worn plaintiveness, and taken together with his melancholic eyes they aided in presenting a character for whom Fortune never spared a smile.

Martin's finely etched cameos go far back. He turns up in *Cowboy*, a cattle drive tale starring Glenn Ford and Jack Lemmon in which he plays the victim of an oafish prank. Cowpunchers attempt to frighten Lemmon, a greenhorn, by tossing a sidewinder at his feet. The pitch strays, landing the snake on Martin, one of the company's more mild-mannered hands. He is bitten in the neck, leaving his companions and the audience with nothing to do but sit in vigil as he slips through delirium into coma and death. Martin portrayed the beleaguered Union sergeant who begged *Shenandoah*'s irate father (played by James Stewart), "Please, Mister. Don't burn my train. It's a *nice* train." He played the shrill sycophant kept in tow by Lee Marvin in *The Man Who Shot Liberty Valance*. In *The Sons of Katie Elder* he was lured away from a poker table by Dean Martin's raffle of a glass eye. Strother wins and is ecstatic, beaming as he plops the prize against the center of his forehead, and gasping, "I always wanted another eye!"

In *True Grit* he shows up as Colonel Stonehill, a slick horsetrader with shrewish spite on tap when a deal turns against him. In *Rooster Cogburn* he crosses paths with the John Wayne character once again, playing a seedy misanthrope who took the job of frontier ferryman to get away from people. In *Butch Cassidy and the Sundance Kid* he is an inoffensive mines paymaster who had adapted to Bolivia by blending into the background, taking on "color," only to be shot off his horse in the middle of "Polly Wolly Doodle." With *Fool's Parade*, having been released from the penitentiary with James Stewart and Kurt Russell, he wants nothing more from life than to work in their projected mercantile store. Throughout the picture he hugs a want-book of items like a security blanket, as it represents for him the peaceful remainder of his misspent existence. In *Red Sky at Morning* he is the trashy father of two high school strumpets. He bursts into his daughters' classroom with a shotgun, demanding a confession from the father of his grandchildren-to-be.

In *Hannie Caulder* he makes the third—with Jack Elam and Ernest Borgnine—of a trio of brothers referred to by one reviewer as the "homicidal Three Stooges." During the rape of Hannie (Raquel Welch), it is Martin who gets tossed out on his duff and told to go mind the horses. In *Sssssss* we find a mad herpetologist bent on creating a human/snake mutation; but a man who in quietude sips whiskey and reads Walt Whitman to his pet reptile, Harry. In *The Wild Bunch* he waxes eloquent, railing, "Liar! Liar! *Black* liar!" to his friend T.C. Yet, he is heartstricken when he recognizes the hurt his words have caused. (Meanwhile, both are oblivious to the carnage their bullets have brought.) In the Depression era of *Hard Times* he is a washed out, unlicensed doctor who has surrendered his body to narcotics and his mind to dreams and speculations. He pulls himself together, however, and proves a street-wise guide through the murk of New Orleans' underworld. In *Great Scout & Cathouse Thursday* he plays a man who cannot know a woman's smile or gentle touch without the exchange of legal tender.

Finally, with a closer look at Cap'n in *Cool Hand Luke*, one notices a fragility. Cap'n addresses new inmates in a paternal, entreating voice. In the evening, when younger, tougher men still perspire, he wears a sweater to ward off a chill. With Strother Martin's characters there always seems to be some frailness, a soft spot, a position on the short end of the stick that makes his villains, sympathetic heavies and off-beats seem not so remote, far from invincible, and sharers of the same infirmities we all suffer. It is this humane touch by Martin that would have earned for him—were coats of arms still designed to honor a thespian for his contributions—a heraldic symbol exclusive to his escutcheon: the koala rampant.

Off-screen, of course, Strother Martin had all the redeeming social graces, including an extra helping of modesty over his own achievements and a generosity of praise for peers in a craft that, clearly, he cared for deeply. What we did *not* have here was a failure to communicate.

I learned first that Martin, like his fellow horseback hellions, had been a Navy veteran. He insisted that he came out as an officer only because they were "scraping the bottom of the barrel" near the end of World War II, and that land-bound ensigns like himself—performing nonhazardous duty in Hawaii for the balance of the war—were dubbed "ball-bearing WAVES," hardly a point to boast.

Before entering the military, Martin had been a college athlete, a piece of information that caught me by surprise.

"A lot of people don't know that about me," Martin said. "I graduated from the University of Michigan majoring in speech and drama. I was Michigan's number one diver, Michigan was national and intercollegiate champion all the time I was there in school, and I made number two national springboard diving champion. My nickname was 'T-Bone' Martin, and I was sort of half-assed famous that way. I've been honored at the Swimmers' Hall of Fame at Fort Lauderdale. I was a guest speaker there one year, saw all of my old coaches, and was made an honorary member of an Olympic team."

"How long did you dive before you decided to give it up?" I asked.

"Eighteen years. Diving is like ballet. It takes an enormous amount of training. I had big competition from Ohio State, and almost won a number of dives. And I was *almost* the AAU number one champion; and I *would* have been a candidate for the Olympic games ... except there were no Olympics between 1936 and 1948. I was second on both springboards in forty-four, and I was third in forty-six; but finally, I'd dived so long, I was afraid if I stayed in and they only took three and I was the fourth, I'd have had tears in my eyes as big as horse turds."

"How did the acting start?"

"Well, I think diving was the first *public* thing I ever did. I used to be very shy, and that was the one thing I could do. I was very poor in public speaking courses—I don't know why—and in fact, I had six years of high school with only 'C' averages. I didn't excel at Michigan in drama until I came back after the war for a semester in summer school, and I found that I was very fascinated with all the Bohemian people from New York that revolved around the campus theater. Now that I wasn't an athlete involved in swimming trips, I could devote time to drama. I was only on the stage a couple of times, but then I knew I wanted to do that ... but it was terribly foolhardy. I was not the hotshot of the school by any manner or means. I would have been skeptical of the people like me that semester in summer school, and I think they were all amazed that I made a living in the craft; but I was very persistent."

"Was there a mentor or some inspiration that either gave you a decisive nudge, or kept you going?"

"I think my decision to be an actor," Martin recalled, "—I didn't know I was going to try to make a living—was shortly after I saw *It's a Wonderful Life* in Ann Arbor. It's one of my favorite films of Jimmy Stewart's, and I talked to him about this. There's a scene where Stewart comes home to his children in that story. You and the audience would understand if he took his own life, because he had a hell of a lot of responsibilities, he's had it *rough*! So when he makes the decision not to do that, when he meets the little man on the bridge and goes home and hugs his children … it wasn't as though he were hugging his own children. It was like he was hugging every child in the world. (I only saw this film once, by the way; but that hug of the kid I won't forget ever, for as long as I live. It was wonderful.) And I thought, 'Jesus Christ! Jimmy Stewart don't care what *he* looks like! Why, he's so lanky, he looks a little grotesque!' So *I* definitely started thinking about being an actor.

"I was working recently and just went to Indiana, Pennsylvania, which is where Jimmy Stewart was born and where his father's hardware store was. I had my picture taken there, a big eleven-by-fourteen. There's a sundial on a pedestal there, and I thought it was very dignified. What a nice choice … not too much … that the city of Indiana had! It said, 'This is the Site of the Hardware Store Owned by Alexander Stewart, Father of Movie Actor James Stewart'." He said, almost in a hush, "Just that simplicity on a nice hunk of—probably Vermont—granite. I like to see an actor honored in just about that way. That's nice!"

"Do you still do live theater?" I asked.

"Not now. Not anymore," he answered with some regret. "We don't have time. The last play I did was with Henry Fonda. We were the third play at the Kennedy Center in Washington. I played Kit Carson in Saroyan's *Time of Your Life*. I would have been in Sam Peckinpah's *The Getaway* if I hadn't done that play. Somebody said long ago that the stage is a very cruel mistress. The pay is very poor. Once in a while now I get some kind of offer to do something in New York but there haven't been any super offers." He checked himself. "Well … not bad … but to change homes, pay those rents… Anyway, what I'm trying to say is, film satisfies me."

"Why is it that so many of your roles have been in the redneck and rustic mold?" I asked.

"I began to make a living I guess about 1954, after I'd been in Hollywood about seven years. Mainly I grew up with television, and specifically with things like *Gunsmoke*. I did seventeen *Gunsmokes* in its first ten years. I did so many Westerns because almost every other show was a Western in those days. That's where you could make a living, so I got a chance to really sharpen my tools in that area. Eventually they tend to hire you on what you've done before. Now, there's a sort of smell of the stable about me, and if it's a dress-up guy, they'll think, 'Oh, I don't believe Strother's right for this.'

"Actually, I'm not a very good horseman. I feel very lucky I haven't got *killed* on 'em, and especially in films like *The Wild Bunch*. I feel like I'm not as typecast as some, but a little too much. They imagine there's more horseshit smell on me than there actually is. I'm a man who likes a Beethoven quartet, a fairly cultured individual interested in arts from all over the world."

"How is it, then, that your parts seem to come across in both action and speech with such a high degree of authenticity?" I questioned. "Many other actors, when they take roles that are far less sophisticated than themselves, fail to be as convincing as you are."

"My father, who only went to the third grade, was a sharecropper from Fayette County, Kentucky," Martin replied fondly, and without the least trace of defensiveness. "He was of a family of fourteen. Not all of them lived. They were born in something very close to a log cabin that was miles from any place, and I believe it's still standing. My father and some of his brothers didn't have a great deal of education. They were dirt farmers, and they made a kind of migration one at a time to Kokomo, Indiana, where I was born.

"Incidentally, my name is from that Kentucky area. There aren't that very many of them. 'Strother' is that old Teutonic word for river. Ironically, my grandfather's name is Lake Martin, which would have been a marvelous professional name for me; and easier to remember, since everybody has gotten balled up with 'Strother.' I didn't change it, though. I didn't know I had a name that suited me. For many years I was 'T-Bone' as springboard diving champion. I guess I just wanted to stick with my real name, but it's been a struggle.

"But I'm often playing parts where I sound like my father. His brother and sisters will tell me, 'My god, you sound and look just like Strod!' Indeed, I look even more like my grandfather. I just saw a photograph of my father's family when they were tall and proud. (When I say 'tall and proud,' they certainly weren't tall. My father was my size.) They looked like many of the characters I've played, and," he cautioned, "I *don't* mean they don't look *intelligent!* They were very respected citizens of Kokomo. They were all tough as nails, and none of them ever lost any fistfights."

"Was the part of Cap'n in *Cool Hand Luke* about the point at which your film career accelerated?" I asked.

"Yes," he agreed. "It's interesting. I was such a TV whore, I jumped from show to show. I was making a living, and didn't pay too much attention to movies; and often when I would be put up for a movie they'd say, 'Yeah, we're kinda looking for a guy like Strother. We may even get a New York actor for this.' In those days, somebody hot off the stage was supposed to be something super, and sometimes they are. Anyhow, the director of *Cool Hand Luke*, Stuart Rosenberg, took a long time before saying, 'Okay, the part's yours'."

134 *Strother Martin*

"How did you feel about your first sizable film role?"

"I don't like anything I've done when I first see it," Martin spoke in a shudder. "I can't bear myself. But when I see something I did ten years ago, I'm a little more forgiving of myself, and then I'm proud of it and I can say, 'You did all right.' Of all the films I've done, *Luke* has a nice vintage quality. Over the years it ages well, and one of the reasons is that Paul's acting was absolutely brilliant in it. Take the scene where he was digging the ditch, the egg scene, or the scene with his mama. People see that picture again and again. And I think *The Wild Bunch* is another. I've seen it seven times over the years, and *Luke* maybe five or six, and I'm proud of them both, and some others."

"Such as?"

"I'm proud of *Butch Cassidy* because, you know, it's a bauble, but a masterpiece of a bauble about a man that's glad to be alive. Paul Newman once called it a Western fairy tale. That sepia still sequence in the middle looked like my mother and dad in their wedding pictures. And if you think *Butch* is not profound, take that bicycle scene, and Katharine Ross says, 'Have you ever thought that it might have been you and I instead of Sundance?' and Paul says, 'Well, you're on my bicycle, and in some parts of the world, that's the same as being married.' I liked that. That's damned good writing by William Goldman, and Paul was dazzling. The director, George Roy Hill, is a master at comedy-drama, and I so looked forward to working with him again in *Slapshot* that I was rolling and tossing with excitement for four weeks before starting it."

"*Luke* not only seemed to boost your own career," I noted, "but several other cast members are quite prominent now. At the time you were making it, had you any feeling that the material was in some way momentous?"

"The writer of *Luke*, Donn Pearce, did two years on a gang," Martin replied. "That film came out of his *guts*. When you begin with something original, there was something about *Luke* that you knew it wasn't just a dreamed up screenplay. There *was* a 'Cool Hand Luke,' Donn said. I don't know if he did those things in the picture, but he did some splendid things. That was Donn's inspiration.

"By the way, I was a friend of Donn's. He said he liked me as an actor — but I wasn't *anything* like the *real* Cap'n. I don't know what else I could have done. I got my ideas from his book. I guess he meant he couldn't be afraid of me. We worked together, I had dinner with him, we had drinks, all kinds of things. It's hard for us to be afraid of one another when we're working. Like, when I see *The Wild Bunch*. I had to see that three or four times before I could begin to have a perspective. That's like seeing all my friends, and I don't know when I'm supposed to be afraid. I know I'm not really seeing the film for the first time."

"What exactly was your analysis of Cap'n?"

"He had absolute power over those men. He didn't even need to carry a weapon. Somebody *handed* me that staff when I hit Paul Newman. I don't remember whether they showed that crossover, but one of the guards handed me that staff because he knew I'd hit Luke with it.

"I think my character saw himself as gentle. He didn't like to do violent things, really. He couldn't understand, but he would do them. He would mete out justice. He wanted a smooth-runnin' camp. He liked to sit and watch the boxing matches. There's a kind of impotency about him. Tony Zerbe said, 'He's so *vacant!*' He was in his own world, a little sick; a deadly, pernicious guy, but in a very gentlemanly way. Courteous."

"How did the director guide your formation of this character?"

"Stuart Rosenberg is a very quiet director, but if you approach the camera, he's the *last* person in the world where you'd march into where that camera is, because he's *working* there. Also, he's apt to whisper into an actor's ear. He might say in a very low monotone, 'We're to do a take in about two minutes when you're ready.' Well, that can scare the *hell* out of you, just like being *screamed* at does! You feel a little ill at ease. And all the way through, one of the things Stu called me — in the nicest way possible, not sarcastically — he'd say, 'Hi ... sweet thing.' He'd tease me; but gently."

"What we got here is a failure to communicate," I quoted. "That's become one of the most repeated lines from probably any picture in the last decade. How did you make that utterance so memorable?"

"I knew we ought to hear that as my most important line. Just before I did that scene, I said, 'Are you ready to shoot?' He said, 'In about two minutes,' and I said, 'Okay!' And to rev myself up inside, I ran about a half block, *hard*, 'cause I wanted my heart pumping inside, my adrenalin goin', my blood pressure, everything pulsating. It began very easy, those lines; but underneath, I was huffin' and puffin'."

"Many of your heavies seem to come from the very bottom rung of humanity," I suggested. "They are either morally obtuse like Cap'n, or vicious and mangy as in *Hannie Caulder* or *The Wild Bunch*. How can you possibly reconcile yourself to a part like that?"

"I don't play very many smoothies," Martin admitted. "I play a lot of characters that have been under a lot of stress — and," he confided, "*I've had* a lot of stress in my life. I didn't make a living for a long time. I think my early shyness came from my being terribly poor. I didn't have a suit and jacket all the way through the University of Michigan, and as a matter of fact I went through high school the same way. The other people around me at the universities and whatnot seemingly always had pocket money, and *I* never had the money for a *coke!* So underneath, when I was young I probably envied the wealthy. I hope I've outgrown that some, because I feel some compassion for those people who were born with a gold spoon in their mouths, and had it yanked out with half their teeth."

"One of the things so horrifying about *The Wild Bunch*," I pursued, "was that not only did it have your traditional shootouts, but innocent civilians got caught in the crossfire, and your and L.Q. Jones's characters went down into the street and looted the dead."

"Yes, I was stealing *little* things like coins and a small crucifix. I think we're getting back to the subject of villainy. I don't try to play a 'bad guy' in a sense," he said. "Coffer does things with a certain amount of *joy*. The only thing he has working for him in his life is his competitiveness and affection for T.C. But I didn't know that when I was doing it, especially. It was after I'd done it and saw it, I said, 'Hell, the little guy *liked* T.C.' And Coffer might kill *him*, but he'd *miss* 'im, because he was somebody to *argue* with."

"What was it like to work with Sam Peckinpah?" I asked.

"He was *fantastic* to work with in this film! I think he told somebody, 'I'm going to make the actors' life hell in this movie,' because he wanted that on the screen. It wasn't really hell," Martin chuckled, "because we had *marvelous* fiestas, and we almost lived the lives of those kinds of characters. Our parties, fiestas, were pretty wild.

"Sam has a short temper, and there's no lethargy on a Peckinpah film. Indeed, there's no lethargy on *any* good director's set. Sam has a way of *destroying* lethargy. I've always said he ate me alive on every goddamn take in that movie. And he never tells you until later that he was kidding you. At the time, there's a mischievous look about Sam's face, a little grin. But he could chew me out until I was mangled and bleeding and it hurt. I think I was about on the edge of a nervous breakdown on every shot.

"A good director," Martin expounded, "like John Ford, Henry Hathaway, George Roy Hill, Peckinpah — I've worked with all of them … (Stuart Rosenberg is very quiet, but *that's* scary too) — but the other four can all cut you off at your *knees*. They're like dirty psychiatrists. Just before the take, they may say something so fucking insulting to you that you think, 'Well, goddamnit, *I* don't have to *take* this!' and they say, '*All-rightquietlet'srollit!*' And while you're in that state of … whatever … you've gotta do that take. Most good directors get us off balance a little bit so that we're not doing just quite what we thought we'd do when we were at home preparing the part. Sam had to keep the set bristling with a certain taut tension. It's a kind of gung-ho Go!-Go!-Go!

"One of the scenes that I was involved with was that scene that started the movie, on the roof. I asked Sam could I wink at L.Q. once. Sam said, '*Why* don't you *kiss 'im?*' He *said* it like he was goin' to *kill* me! In a moment, when he's talking me through one little close-up where I kiss that rifle" — the choke of disgust could be heard in Martin's voice — "that was *his* idea. I thought, 'I don't want to *do* that,' but he told me during the take, 'All right. Kiss that gun. *Kiss* it *again, goddamnit!*' He had hurt me so bad just before the take that underneath, I'm quivering.

"I realize now what's happening to me when a director's working in that way. All good directors see through us like a piece of glass. They know where your psyche is, or they make damned good guesses about it.

If they think an insult is going to bring out the psychotic side of you more, then they'll lay one into you and some of them are *beauties*. I've seen grown men cry—and then go do beautiful performances. All good directors play psychological games with us. They manipulate us, and it begins to smart sometimes.

"My own attitude about all good directors; they look at the rehearsal as important; but the *take* ... I don't know what other word to say except it's 'sacred.' When they've got film in that camera, you should really be trying to *do* it. Everything else don't mean shit. And at this moment you hope—in the case of *The Wild Bunch*—will I really *see* L.Q.? Will I really look and see what he is, sum total as a human being?

"My answer is, yes. I remember a certain moment seeing a look on L.Q.'s face that I'd never seen before. If you pray for super-concentration at that point, and if you get *really* interested in what the *other* person's doing and you forget all about yourself, and if you don't know what *you* did, quite, and if you think, 'Goddamn, *they* were *terrific!*' when the take is over ... then you probably did all right."

As an afterthought, Martin added, "I said to you Sam's never said anything good to me? I saw that little twisted grin once in a while, especially when he made me smart. But he never said *anything* was worth a crap until the damn movie was over. We were going to Warner Brothers to do some looping on it and he turned to me and said off-handedly, 'By the way. You're very good in this picture.' I think he had a good time doing it. He'd get L.Q. and me arguing like hell with one another. L.Q. might explain what Sam was trying to say, then I'd get to raising hell with him. We just worked out well together."

"I believe that interplay carried over into the buffoonery of your two characters," I commented, "which offered welcome comic relief from the gore and violence. Unfortunately, it was that violence that drew so much return-fire from the critics. What kind of reactions have you personally run into?"

"Sometimes out here they have a screening of it and I get invited. People that know it say, 'Strother, we're going to have a screening at 12:30 at such-and-such a theater and they'd like to see you there.' The last time I went to a screening, I was with Warren Oates in the middle of the night. I don't mean a grand affair. The screening may be some neighborhood theater ... but somebody says, '*The Wild Bunch* is showing!' and the word spreads like wildfire. Sam had a screening three years ago at the Beverly Canon. The whole theater was *filled* with the friends of that film. When I say 'friends,' I mean some of them are Ph.D.'s in film, some of them are Hell's Angels type of guys. And you run into people that say, 'I've seen it thirty-two times, man. Greatest Western ever made!' Now, I don't know if that's true or not, but that's the kind of comment I've heard over and over again. I've gone to theaters where people come out to touch you, to tell you they liked it. Some have seen it thirty, forty, fifty times. I've seen it seven times, and every time, I see something new. It's really an epic film. To me, Sam is miles above his material. He had a fair-to-good script going in; but the tapestry behind it is the birth of Mexico. That background is just fantastic. I've seen the uncut version, and my appreciation of that has grown each time I go."

"You mentioned John Ford. How did you happen to work for him? Wasn't that on *Liberty Valance?*"

"No," Martin replied, "I did a tiny bit in *The Horse Soldiers* first, and that's when I met him; and he liked me, I guess. Ford said to somebody I knew, 'I've got to get something else for that Stuffer ... Smucker ... Stoofer ... *whatever* the hell his name is,' and he put me in *The Man Who Shot Liberty Valance.* Now Ford," he said darkly, "is the wizard of *all time* as far as seeing through you like a piece of glass; and we have one other that's very similar to him, and I can't praise him highly enough, Henry Hathaway. John Ford said to me one day—he knew that I was scared to death of him—he said, 'I'm going to tell Henry Hathaway about you. Henry,' and he smacked his lips like a French chef, 'would have a l-o-t of fu-n-nn with you.' And when I got my first call for Hathaway, I didn't want to do it, I thought. Legends about how tough he was, and how salty his language was, had scared the hell out of me. I was *afraid* of him. Well, it worked out fine, I just loved him. And I'd been at the same salary for, oh, many years until he gave me my first raise, on *True Grit.* He *doubled* my salary!"

Mindful of Martin's admiration for James Stewart, I said, "Working on *Liberty Valance* must have been quite an event for you."

"I didn't get to know Stewart then, because he was having his own—what will I say?—his own 'experience' working with Duke and with John Ford; and my own scenes weren't with him except that one steak scene. I worked with him again in *Shenandoah* and discussed *It's a Wonderful Life* with him, and I came to realize he liked that film very much, too."

"You played the leads in *The Brotherhood of Satan* and *Sssssss.* Being that you were the star of both films, and each had a prevalent element of the supernatural, was it this element that attracted you to the material?"

Martin seemed taken aback by my abrupt down-shift from inquiring after Ford and Hathaway to pursuing less auspicious films in his career. "I accepted them because they were a challenge at the time, and the work that was available to me," he said. "Interestingly enough, they have both done well at the box office. Not *super*, but both are in the black. The scripts, you know, are not the easiest thing in the world to deal with," he said pointedly. "It's kind of hard to save your ass in some of those situations; like, changing the boy into a snake ain't gonna get too many Ph.D.'s in there. And these were lower budget films. We spent three weeks on *Sssssss.* That's all. Ironically, I got one review of *Brotherhood of*

Satan that said, 'Strother Martin entertains himself and nobody else' ... which kind of smarts a little. But I'm not ashamed of either of those films. I did the best I could with the amount of time I had."

"Were you comfortable working with the snakes?"

"Oh, good God!" Martin gasped. "During the time I was there ... more or less, yes. I was about as wary as anybody else, and the fear comes back again; but I wasn't edgy. To look a king cobra in the eye is a unique experience, because they look at you like a reporter looks at you, or a policeman. They follow you with their eyes. Other snakes kind of hug to the ground and they're not looking at anything, but a king cobra comes up and says hello. We had a snake man on the picture, but I handled a lot of the snakes for real. I was bitten on purpose by that one little blue racer that was stimulating the black mambo; but the director asked, 'Would I?' because I had to say dialogue right after that bite, unburden myself onto my pet snake Harry."

"Would you like to have more films of your own?"

"You mean, to be a lead?" he asked, not sounding too deeply stirred by the proposition. "No, not necessarily. I just like to do good parts. I like all kinds of work. It doesn't matter."

As "good parts" go, one need look no farther than the character Poe in *Hard Times* as evidence of Martin's craftsmanship in projecting the outré. It was not only a plum of a character role, but down off a horse for a change, and in terms of on-camera exposure it made him nearly an equal partner with stars Charles Bronson and James Coburn in a very underrated, grittily charming film. Since we had touched on the emotional bases for some of his screen down-and-outs—the kind of quirks much depended on by self-proclaimed "serious" actors—Martin referred to Poe to remind me that exterior transformations are just as important for a good actor in making his visual statement.

"My hair is almost completely white now," he said, "but when one is doing a heavy or some off-color character, he seldom has light or blond hair. He looks too much like a minister. Actors have a way of knocking that lightness down. They can have it either dingy or dyed. In *Hard Times*, I had it dyed black, and wanted it to *look* dyed, to look like the *cheapest* dye job on the charts. I was really aiming for a resemblance to Edgar Allan Poe, but people interpreted the character as looking like Tennessee Williams." Recalling *Hard Times* also prompted Martin to describe a mixed blessing for actors: behind-the-scenes knowledge of a movie shooting. Evidently the public, privy only to the released edition, can never despair over how many ways the final product could have been different. "Poe said he was on opium. He was very candid and that's why Bronson's character bought him. But they cut all kinds of things out, shortened it about twenty-five minutes. A scene where I went for my connection was cut. They cut on both Coburn and me, which I have nothing against; but I wish they hadn't, it was a good part."

"Weren't you satisfied with the picture?" I asked.

"Well, it's done very well financially," Martin said with some hesitation, "but ... sometimes when we do films they edit things down; and I think the way they edited *Sssssss*, the audience was confused a little about what they were supposed to think. I believe the editors trimmed a lot of things at the beginning because they were in such a hurry to show the snakes. You know, a film is a collective effort of a lot of things. They'll say it's a director's medium — which it is, especially — but sometimes the editor will say, 'Let's lose this sequence or that one.' Where they've cut out twenty-five minutes of the story they shot, as they did in *Hard Times*, the design of things has changed around considerably and you may not look the same. For example, you'll remember when Coburn went to the whorehouse. Well, that was supposed to follow a sequence where his girl had split for Miami; and he didn't have a girlfriend, so he was trying to satisfy his loneliness and need by going to the whorehouse; but because the editors leave out the sequence where they split up, you didn't know why Coburn was there when he had a perfectly good girlfriend.

"More specifically, let me tell you about something involving me. Many years ago I did a film called *Sanctuary*, Faulkner's story. I played a character, 'Dog Boy,' and they explain in the script that my character had a larynx difficulty — either by operation or whatever — and he couldn't speak above a whisper. They were coming back to the rumrunner's shack and Lee Remick asked me, 'Where can we get the booze?' and I said something to her in a raspy whisper. Then her character said to me, 'What's wrong with your voice;' and mine answered, 'Ain't nothin' wrong with muh voice. Ah cain't make much noise, that's all.' Well, they cut out the lines after and including 'What's wrong with your voice?' so I talk in a raspy whisper all through the picture, and you don't know why. We had no control over that," he groused. "A lot of people have their hands in the soup in a film."

Because of his track record, an Oscar nomination did not seem improbable some day, so I asked Martin, as I did his friend L.Q., if he would be a willing recipient or a holdout. "Not at all," he scoffed at the latter. "I think it's very nice, I mean, I'd feel very honored. I don't think actors should compete with one another, but of course I would accept a nomination. If I did get it, I wouldn't turn it down. But I don't think about that at all. For example, though, I think about the film. Not *me*, but the *film*. Like when we were doing *Cool Hand Luke*, we knew we were doing a good film, that it would probably get considered. You sensed that in the air. That's very exciting, when you think you're in a film that might be of great merit."

"Have you *never* felt an Oscar was forthcoming for something you did?" I pressed.

"Never. I try not to think about that. I try to shove that out of my skull. I always think it would be kind of nice," he chuckled, "to be nominated, and *lose*; so that people the rest of your life said, '*You* should have *won* it'!"

"Out of your nearly three decades of work as an actor on the stage, on television and in the movies — outside of the financial rewards — what has it meant to you?"

The man who started poor, who had lived under great stress, who years ago had foregone the security of regular wages to cast his lot against great odds, chasing the phantom of *success* as an actor, replied thoughtfully in the low purr that was uniquely Strother Martin's. "Lee Marvin," he began, "said to me, when we were doin' *Liberty Valance*, something like, 'You know, we play all kinds of people as actors: psychopaths, sexually awry, screwed up — all kinds of humanity. We laughingly go home and say, "What the hell? It's just a character"!' Lee's hand came up on my shoulder and he looked me right in the eye and said ... 'It's *you*, baby.'

"Do you understand?" Martin paused, letting that indictment sink in. "It's *you*. My own feeling is that it's some *part* of you. Maybe a little aspect put up to the hundredth power on the microscope; but it's some part of you. It's interesting. About a profession, I feel we are the finest. If Euripides was alive, he'd be writing for television and movies. Shakespeare would write for television and movies. Ibsen would write for them, Shaw ... some of the finest minds that have existed in our civilization have written for the theater or for audiences and said, 'This is what humanity is like.' All actors in their studies go through these classic plays over and over again. And it's a tough assignment for an actor, because he has to go out in that twilight zone and have his psyche out to the reaches of where it's ... it's hairy. You can run into your own *madness* out there; and after you finish the part, you have to come *back* into a kind of everyday life. It can scare *hell* out of you.

"I've found a lot of things about the emotional side of me. It's been a fantastic voyage of discovery; and some of it is like turning over a rock and seeing a lot of squirmy things you wish weren't there. But they are something like some part of you, or it's no good. I said to a doctor once a long time ago, 'In other people I see their merits, their weak points, bad points, their goodness and their villainy. In most people I see a little sparkle of diamond dust and glitter; and,' I said, 'I suppose there's some diamond dust with me ... but in so much shit, it don't have much luster.'

"Well, I feel very honored ... for example, you're a younger man than me, and your generation accepts me as if I am 'now' as an actor. And I'm an old guy, I'm fifty-eight. And there's a cult for me — everybody don't like me — but there's a few voices, and you're one of them, out there in the woods that say, 'Hey! He's *doin'* it, and he rings *true*!' And since you've seen so much film — much, much more than I'd seen when I was your age — I feel very honored there's several of you out there that like me and go see what I'm trying to do. And I say sometimes, this younger generation with their television set in front of them dishing out pablum, many of them have grown up and watched me twenty-three years, and *still* don't spin the dial when they see me! Some people detest me, I'm sure. They'll say, 'Oh, there's that mealy-mouthed bastard!' or whatever. But some of them say, 'I've liked you ever since I was a child.' So, I go on tryin' to do the best I can. I like to go on surprising them if I can with other aspects of me; and at the same time, I surprise and—if you like—scare the livin' hell out of myself as I learn new things about me, doing each part."

"Strother," I concluded, "you've had some of your finest hours working in films. Or to put it a better way, film has gotten some of its finest hours from *you*. You said before that that medium satisfies you, more than do theater and television. Why?"

"It's a joy to work movies because the material is apt to be a little different, and there's a little more time. And that big screen ... when the movie's great, it's *super!*

"When film is good," he exulted, "it's like *church* to us. I mean, it's like we've had a good sermon. A film that did that for me was *Midnight Cowboy*. When you first meet those people in *Cowboy*, Ratso Rizzo and Joe Buck, you wouldn't give 'em floor space in your house. You'd be *scared* of them. But when you realize the tons of pressure-per-square-inch on both of them, by the time the movie is over you'd go down the street to get a box of cough drops for Ratso Rizzo, or you might give him your coat— because that's such a superb film! In a sense, it's like a Chekhov play. In a Chekhov play everybody's got to get to Moscow or they're gonna die. In *Midnight Cowboy*, they've got to make it to Miami or they can't live. Tuberculosis is gonna kill Ratso if he doesn't get to warm climate. And the thing that's beautiful, and I've said this before, once or twice: If it's your super dream," Martin stated bluntly, "nobody ever really gets to Miami. But," he softened the blow, "the human animal looks very beautiful when he's trying; and if he does everything to the best of his ability, maybe he gets to the suburbs, and the palm tree shadows will come swinging across his face ... when he buys the farm." [June 1976.]*

On August 1, 1980, Strother Martin died of a heart attack suffered at his home in Agoura, California.

VI
Before the Credits Roll

One Friday evening in 1969, your narrator returned — cinematically speaking — to the womb. I visited the Inglewood Theater where I am told I saw my very first movie in 1951. The Cavalry and the Indians initiated me into the vast fraternity of avid moviegoers on that occasion, and I am given to understand that for such a little tyke, I enjoyed it very much. Although I couldn't corroborate, it sounds just like me.

On the forementioned evening in 1969 I had come to see *Gone with the Wind* for probably the third time. The Inglewood, a gigantic old neighborhood theater, had nearly filled its 1,100-seat capacity. Few theaters can hope any longer to reach such figures consistently, which explains the current proliferation of tri- and quad-cinemas with 200–400 seat halls. It also explains why the Inglewood is now a salvage furniture showroom. But on that evening thirteen years ago it was family night. There would be no school next day, so the kids had come along with the older generation, and the Inglewood was packed.

Gone with the Wind is not for everyone. I have met its detractors, but I have seen as many skeptical first-timers come to scoff and walk away converted. It is the quintessential American Movie. Reams have been printed analyzing why it is deemed so, but on the night in question *GWTW* provided me a first-hand insight not only into its own power but, by inference, into the power of the motion picture medium.

There is a scene at the Wilkeses' mansion, Twelve Oaks, when Scarlett O'Hara and another coquette ascend a winding staircase. Her friend relates the scandalous reputation of one Rhett Butler and, as Scarlett looks down at the selfsame rake, he returns her gaze from the bottom of the stairs. It is here we see one of the greatest camera zooms of all time. The strength of Clark Gable's effortless appeal is captured here better than anywhere else as he leans against the bannister, leers up at a new prospect for conquest, and his image gradually fills the screen. It is one magnificent take. At this point that evening inside the Inglewood, something occurred that I had never witnessed before. When the crowd caught sight of Gable for the first time, there was an indescribable sound that issued from it, a collective gasp — or a sigh — or a rapid catching of breath — or a rush of white noise; or perhaps it was a sensation, like hitting an air pocket, or sudden decompression. Whatever it was, the audience was perceivably transfixed. The King *had* them. It could not be allayed to the number of his female contemporaries who were present. To be sure, many were there; but so were their husbands, as well as teen-agers, college kids, young marrieds. In short, the audience was a representative cross-section of every age and social group sufficiently mature and rational to respond to what was on screen; and respond it did. Thirty years after *GWTW's* initial release, Clark Gable had simply knocked the wind out of one more crowd of people, and he strung them along all the way to frankly telling the Southern belle of his dreams that he didn't give a damn.

One winter evening in 1979 I was awarded another persuasive revelation, this time at the campus cinema of the college where I had been a junior ten years before. The bill offered a double feature. For this screening hall, it was an extremely incongruous one, sandwiched as it was between Fellini and Bergman mini-festivals, followed by the latest from Wertmuller, Bertolucci, and Woody Allen. I was a fan, however, and had come to relish *A Fistful of Dollars* and *For a Few Dollars More*, despite the hoots and jeers I fully expected them to be greeted with in this haven of sophistication and intellect.

It never dawned on me that the students who had come to the showing would be watching the film afresh. Their reactions would not be biased by the opprobrium reserved for the spaghetti Western, because that genre's heyday had, for the most part, preceded their years of active, voluntary movie attendance. Its ill fame lay totally outside their directly acquired film awareness. Unless their parents had escorted them to the R-rated features, it is unlikely they ever saw the films on their initial runs, as *Fistful* and *Few* were released when the students were anywhere be-tween four and ten years of age. Perhaps in the interim they may have caught one or the other on television, but it is almost certain they had never been immersed in both, in full color on the big screen, at one sit-ting.

When I saw young men and women heading for the exits, staring ahead, silent, or speaking in short bursts, jerking their shoulders, or laughing nervously, I knew they had been jarred. Seeing this confirmed my faith in the first two *Dollars* installments as captivating pieces of cinema. During certain scenes when one would expect a modern gathering of youth—nurtured during its formative years on passivity, sensitivity, social concern, caring, and the power of positive sarcasm over brute force—to bolt from the room in protest, these young adults sat in rapt attention. They were watching a form of entertainment they had never seen before. If something held them there, against the influence of all the antiviolence diatribes they had been subjected to for half their lives, then what held them in place, in some way, had to have validity.

There was one other benefit I derived from watching a replay of the two Leone Westerns. In the long months prior, during the researching and writing of this book, I had often encountered the antithesis to its thesis; enough times to make me wonder if perhaps I really had nothing here at all, that actually I had *not* selected a group of very fine actors and under-appreciated movies to discuss. Perhaps *Fistful* and *For a Few Dollars More* had been deservedly written off as transplanted horse operas, that their principal performers were truly guilty of merely grunting or mouthing their lines, and rather bullishly plodding through. But when I saw *For a Few Dollars More* again for the first time in years, I was delighted at the lightness of touch in Lee Van Cleef's portrayal of Colonel Mortimer, the many subtleties he employed to convey the character as only an actor of skill could do. I presumed this would be the case, of course, although in the ensuing years only the starkest impressions of the film had survived; but when it was over, I was certain. It confirmed all I had written about Van Cleef, and restored confidence in my powers of recall in his respect, and respecting other actors and films. Consequently, I was emboldened to finish this work, disclose it to my fellow enthusiasts of the cinema, and draw the following conclusions.

It is reassuring, for one, to find all our heavies, shrunk from twenty feet tall down to life-size, to be accessible, congenial, and guilty of nothing worse than making — by the standards of their industry — a decent, middle-income living. A shortfall in megabucks is partly compensated by recurrent demands on their uncommon powers of persuasion. They routinely snare us into an on-screen experience by convincing us of the truth of what we see at a given moment. Sometimes that experience is sordid, sometimes it is ugly, and sometimes it is revolting, but in the preceding chapters our subjects have stood up well to charges that this is a corrupting influence, and their words give rise to another observation.

Oddly enough, we began in Chapter One with a comparison of religious ritual to motion pictures, and came full circle to Strother Martin's notion that movies can be "like church to us," like a "good sermon." His analogy is appropriate for many of the films alluded to in this volume, not because of their genteel exposition of divine or humanist graces, but rather for the harsh lessons they bear regarding mankind. Sermons are meant not only to challenge the intellect with ethical brain-teasers, but to edify, to provide a wayward life some direction, to make a difference. On these terms, does the analogy still hold? Apparently so. Martin himself is proof positive of how a single movie can change the course of a man's affairs. Frank Capra's *It's a Wonderful Life*, like a giant "I Want You" poster, reached out into an Ann Arbor audience and recruited an obscure drama student into the ranks of theatrical and screen performers; a student whose chances for major success were as minute as those of most actors-to-be. It led to a career and a body of work for which any actor could be proud. The film itself told how a single man's life counted for something in the general scheme around him, allowing a dismal glimpse of the puzzle with his own piece missing. Schmaltz? Try to recall Strother

Martin's major films since his breakthrough in *Cool Hand Luke*, deduct the unique flair he contributed to them, and Capra's point is well taken.

Of course, *It's a Wonderful Life* ended cheerfully, offering a welcome uplift that is sure to console audiences for generations to come. It wins an easy seal of approval and does not fit our profile of badness at the Bijou. But in a roundabout way, it does suggest an apologia for movies that defame us as a species.

Can it be so wonderful a life, after all, that has to end in a heap in Guyana, denuded and strangled on a Los Angeles hillside, limed and buried in a suburban Chicago crawlspace, or butchered in a New Mexico prison? As part of a general trend these days to decry "gratuitous" violence in movies and television, is it fair in the process to snub men who portray the seamier aspects of man, and to write them off for degrading human existence in their work? Not in the least. They are at fault only in fiction. A *character* is doing it. Him. Not Bill McKinney or L.Q. Jones. Not Lee Van Cleef or Andrew Robinson, but that *character*. *Him!* *He's* doing it! That pattern of light shot through a razor-thin photographic emulsion and onto a screen, that figure that scampers now into the wings or collapses dead into the Bijou's old organ pit. *He's* the one that's guilty — and who is he but a pale reflection of real boosters of our soaring crime statistics?

No matter how repellent the violence has been in motion pictures and television for the last couple of decades, none has equalled in horror or been so graphic as actual events reported in recent years. No matter how devastating a cinematic predicament is to a character in a movie, it has a worse counterpart in real life. Watching a heavy in action is a reminder of these sad truths. Whether he is an incidental nuisance who cannot muster the grit to overcome his own inertia and remove himself from the paths of others, or he is an amusing sympathetic heavy who ultimately makes for uneasy company, or he is a thoroughbred villain with blood-dripping hands, the heavy constantly herds us into heroic company, forces us to lift our sights ever higher and to make the best choices in a given situation.

Our prime concerns are no longer seasonal changes, demons, or some personified generality like "Flesh" or "Death." Modern life is full of minor aggravations as the result of slipshod, insensitive, unstable elements in our midst; and we now worry more immediately about crooked politicians, unsafe streets, homes that cannot be left unsecured, and possessions that could disappear in an instant at the whim of ruthless hoodlums. If, in the long run, an actor-heavy persuades us that exploiting the weak and defenseless is an atrocity, that the exercise of power for its own sake is insanity, and that a penchant for easy pickings and going with the flow is cowardice, and he keeps a fire of indignation burning in the face of all these things; then, at this interval in our history — where is the disservice?

Among the actors who have contributed so generously to this survey there is one common factor. Whatever they do — to put it vaguely — "works." It cannot be described more precisely. An aspiring actor who hopes to emulate their level of success in the performing arts cannot rest on the assurance that he hails from a particular spot on the map or earns his rent and meals by a special trade, or that he has reached a certain rung on the ladder of formal education, studied at some prestigious institution, widened his preparation for the entertainment field to cover as many areas as possible, or narrowed his scope to only one or two areas of expertise. We have heard from natives of New England, the South, the Midwest, and the Southwest; high school dropouts and holders of graduate degrees; strangers to the stage, and a former student in the Bard's city; an ex-cowboy, an ex-accountant, an ex-dishwasher, an ex-career soldier caught short; an actor-comedy writer, an actor-singer, an actor-painter, and men who confine their talents strictly to making film and television appearances. Whatever drew them from different regions, backgrounds and disciplines, no pat success formula can be distilled except to say that what they do "works."

Chance, it seems, has played a significant hand in ushering this collection of actors to the Bijou, and in keeping them there for our enjoyment. Had Jack Elam managed to save his injured eye in that fateful childhood accident, he would probably be running his own accounting firm today. World War II might have claimed the life of Neville Brand, or Lee Van Cleef, or Strother Martin. Old schoolmate Fess Parker's copy of *Battle Cry* could have missed the plane to L.Q. Jones in Nicaragua. In the filming process, too, so many individual efforts converge in every take. All the possible variations in each effort interpolate into a million different ways a scene could be shot; but spliced in sequence together with the rest, they all arrive at the Bijou in a version that "works," according to the judgment of dozens of craftsmen. Finally, an accumulation of scenes and movies that happen to achieve merit in the eyes of the public or the film industry will sustain an actor's career. It is not *all* chance, of course. Diligent application on the job, refresher training off the job, keeping physically fit, jockeying for the main chance, procuring sage advice, and establishing useful connections figure into most success stories. As we have seen, they have much to do with the events recorded here.

For the company assembled here, a quest for gainful employment continues. Where will we see them next? A lot depends on the trends of the mid 1980's. Will we see even more films and teledramas on the problems of courtship, marriage and divorce? More outer space adventure? A less heated perspective on the civil rights struggle or the Vietnam War? More lawyer and journalist heroes armed with briefcase and notepad? A revival of the Western? The musical? Whatever the case, surely the new trends will offer an abundance of villains, updated to fit the spirit of the day.

At the same time, a new decade will call for fresh faces. Not fresh in the sense of youthful, necessarily; fresh in the sense of novel. Strong, experienced, magnetic actors must come to the fore, and assume lead roles in partnership with — or in displacement of — the sixties' and seventies' shopworn discoveries. Up to this point, the stories accounted herein lie off the beaten path of Tinseltown reportage. They cannot boast of super-stardom, super agents, or multimillion dollar deals hashed out in posh Hollywood eateries. But lightning can strike anywhere, and if it favored one of the actors self-revealed in these pages, well ... it couldn't happen to a nicer fellow.

Assuredly, it is a comfort to meet Elam and Brand, McKinney, Donner and the rest on a personal basis, away from the unsettling, frightening impressions their performances have made on us. Confronting them in this way allows us to see the starting point of a fiendish charac-terization — the actor, a person not too unlike ourselves. Putting this together with our recollection of the moral and emotional depths they have visited before the cameras, however, leads us to recognize — perhaps reluctantly, if we didn't beforehand — the obligations of their calling. They are like reporters recording the truth about human nature, *our* nature, in all its facets. About our common humanity there is good news, and there is bad news. For movies they have incarnated the violence and menace that everyone fears. They have breathed life into mayhem, per-versions, and vicious acts that began as paper fictions, and they have made them seem undeniably real. More disturbingly, the sense of that reality infects us with a terrible notion that those flaws, weaknesses, and savage impulses played out on screen can be found on the worst side of us all. That's the bad news. But just as it would be to our detriment to ignore daily news accounts on external events that shape our lives, it is good for us to know of those malformed internal shapes that escape from man and play havoc. That is a service the heavies provide; we are far better off for watching them.

Filmography

Luke Askew

1967 *The Happening* (Columbia), *Hurry Sundown* (Paramount), *Cool Hand Luke* (Warner Bros.–Seven Arts)
1968 *The Green Berets* (Warner Bros.–Seven Arts), *The Devil's Brigade* (United Artists), *Will Penny* (Paramount)
1969 *Easy Rider* (Columbia), *Flareup* (MGM)
1970 *Angel Unchained* (American International)
1972 *The Great Northfield, Minnesota Raid* (Universal), *The Culpepper Cattle Company* (20th Century–Fox)
1973 *The Magnificent Seven Ride* (United Artists)
1974 *Slipstream* (Pacific Rim), *Pat Garrett & Billy the Kid* (MGM)
1975 *Posse* (Paramount), *Walking Tall II* (Cinerama/American-International)
1976 *Mackintosh & T.J.* (Penland)
1977 *Rolling Thunder* (American-International)
1979 *Wanda Nevada* (United Artists)

Neville Brand

1949 *D.O.A.* (United Artists)
1951 *The Halls of Montezuma* (20th Century–Fox), *Only the Valiant* (Warner Bros.), *The Mob* (Columbia)
1952 *Red Mountain* (Paramount), *Flame of Araby* (Universal)
1953 *Stalag 17* (Paramount), *Charge at Feather River* (Warner Bros.), *Man Crazy* (20th Century–Fox), *Gun Fury* (Columbia)
1954 *Riot in Cell Block 11* (Allied Artists), *Lone Gun* (United Artists), *Prince Valiant* (20th Century–Fox), *Return from the Sea* (Allied Artists)
1955 *The Prodigal* (MGM), *The Return of Jack Slade* (Allied Artists), *Bobby Ware Is Missing* (Allied Artists)
1956 *Love Me Tender* (20th Century–Fox), *Fury at Gunsight Pass* (Columbia), *Mohawk* (20th Century–Fox), *Raw Edge* (Universal)
1957 *The Way to the Gold* (20th Century–Fox), *Tin Star* (Paramount)
1958 *Cry Terror* (MGM)
1959 *Five Gates to Hell* (20th Century–Fox)

(Neville Brand, *cont.*)

1960 *The Scarface Mob* (Desilu), *The Adventures of Huckleberry Finn* (MGM)
1961 *The George Raft Story* (Allied Artists), *The Last Sunset* (Universal-International)
1962 *Hero's Island* (United Artists), *The Birdman of Alcatraz* (United Artists)
1965 *That Darn Cat* (Buena Vista)
1968 *Three Guns for Texas* (Universal)
1969 *The Desperadoes* (Columbia), *Backtrack* (Universal)
1970 *Tora! Tora! Tora!* (20th Century–Fox)
1972 *The Train Robbers* (Warner Bros.)
1973 *Cahill, U.S. Marshal* (Warner Bros.), *The Deadly Trackers* (Warner Bros.), *The Police Connection* (Cinemation), *This Is a Hijack* (Fanfare), *The Mad Bomber* (Cinemation)
1974 *Scalawag* (Paramount)
1975 *The Psychic Killer* (Avco Embassy)
1978 *Eaten Alive* (Virgo International)
1979 *Hi-Riders* (Dimension), *The Mouse and His Child* [voice] (Sanrio)
1979 *Five Days from Home* (Universal)
1980 *Without Warning* (Filmways)
1981 *Twinkle, Twinkle, Killer Caine* (UFD)

Robert Donner

1963 *The Nutty Professor* (Paramount)
1964 *The Disorderly Orderly* (Paramount)
1966 *Agent for H.A.R.M.* (Universal)
1967 *Catalina Caper* (Crown International), *Cool Hand Luke* (Warner Bros.–Seven Arts), *El Dorado* (Paramount), *The Spirit Is Willing* (Paramount)
1968 *The Private Navy of Sgt. O'Farrell* (United Artists), *Skidoo* (Paramount)
1969 *The Undefeated* (20th Century–Fox)
1970 *Chisum* (Warner Bros.), *Rio Lobo* (National General), *Zig Zag* (MGM)
1971 *Vanishing Point* (20th Century–Fox)
1972 *Mrs. Pollifax, Spy* (United Artists), *Fool's Parade* (Columbia), *something big* (National General)
1973 *The Man Who Loved Cat Dancing* (MGM), *High Plains Drifter* (Universal), *Santee* (Crown International)
1975 *Bite the Bullet* (Columbia), *Take a Hard Ride* (20th Century–Fox)
1977 *The Last Hard Men* (20th Century–Fox)
1979 *Five Days from Home* (Universal)

Jack Elam

1950 *The Sundowners* (Eagle Lion), *One Way Street* (Universal), *American Guerilla in the Phillipines* (20th Century–Fox), *High Lonesome* (United Artists)

1951 *Rawhide* (20th Century–Fox), *Bird of Paradise* (20th Century–Fox)

1952 *Lure of the Wilderness* (20th Century–Fox), *My Man and I* (MGM), *Rancho Notorious* (RKO Radio), *High Noon* (United Artists)

1953 *Kansas City Confidential* (United Artists), *Appointment in Honduras* (RKO Radio), *The Moonlighter* (Warner Bros.), *Gun Belt* (United Artists), *Ride, Vaquero* (MGM), *Count the Hours* (RKO Radio)

1954 *Vera Cruz* (United Artists)

1955 *Artists and Models* (Paramount), *Kismet* (MGM), *The Man from Laramie* (Columbia), *Moonfleet* (MGM), *The Far Country* (Universal), *Cattle Queen of Montana* (RKO Radio)

1956 *Jubal* (Columbia)

1957 *Dragoon Wells Massacre* (Allied Artists), *Gunfight at the OK Corral* (Paramount), *Night Passage* (Universal), *Baby Face Nelson* (United Artists)

1958 *Gun Runners* (United Artists)

1959 *Edge of Eternity* (Columbia)

1961 *The Last Sunset* (MGM), *The Comancheros* (20th Century–Fox), *Pocketful of Miracles* (United Artists)

1962 *4 for Texas* (Warner Bros.)

1966 *Night of the Grizzly* (Paramount), *The Rare Breed* (Universal)

1967 *The Last Challenge* (MGM), *The Way West* (United Artists)

1968 *Firecreek* (Warner Bros.–Seven Arts), *Never a Dull Moment* (Buena Vista)

1969 *Support Your Local Sheriff* (United Artists), *Once Upon a Time in the West* (Paramount)

1970 *The Cockeyed Cowboys of Calico County* (Universal), *Dirty Dingus Magee* (MGM), *Rio Lobo* (National General)

1971 *The Last Rebel* (Columbia), *The Wild Country* (Buena Vista), *Support Your Local Gunfighter* (United Artists)

1972 *Hannie Caulder* (Paramount)

1973 *Pat Garrett & Billy the Kid* (MGM)

1974 *A Knife for the Ladies* (Bryanston)

1976 *Hawmps* (Mulberry Square), *Pony Express Rider* (Doty–Dayton), *Creature from Black Lake* (Howco International), *The Winds of Autumn* (Howco International)

1978 *Gray Eagle* (American-International)

1979 *The Villain* (Columbia), *The Apple Dumpling Gang Rides Again* (Buena Vista), *The Norseman* (American-International)

1981 *Cannonball Run* (20th Century–Fox)

Bo Hopkins

1969 *The Wild Bunch* (Warner Bros.–Seven Arts), *The Bridge at Remagen* (United Artists), *The 1,000 Plane Raid* (United Artists)
1970 *Monte Walsh* (National General), *Macho Callahan* (Avco–Embassy), *The Moonshine War* (MGM)
1972 *The Culpepper Cattle Company* (20th Century–Fox), *The Getaway* (National General), *The Only Way Home* (Regional)
1973 *White Lightning* (United Artists), *The Man Who Loved Cat Dancing* (MGM), *American Graffiti* (Universal)
1975 *The Nickel Ride* (20th Century–Fox), *The Day of the Locust* (Paramount), *Posse* (Paramount), *The Killer Elite* (United Artists)
1976 *A Small Town in Texas* (American-International)
1977 *Tentacles* (American-International)
1978 *Midnight Express* (Columbia)
1979 *More American Graffiti* (Universal)
1981 *The Fifth Floor* (Film Ventures International)

L.Q. Jones

1955 *Battle Cry* (Warner Bros.), *An Annapolis Story* (Allied Artists), *Target Zero* (Warner Bros.)
1956 *Santiago* (Warner Bros.), *Toward the Unknown* (Warner Bros.)
1957 *Operation Mad Ball* (Columbia)
1958 *The Young Lions* (20th Century–Fox), *The Naked and the Dead* (Warner Bros.), *Torpedo Run* (MGM)
1960 *Flaming Star* (20th Century–Fox)
1962 *Ride the High Country* (MGM), *Hell Is for Heroes* (Paramount)
1963 *Showdown* (Universal)
1964 *Apache Rifles* (20th Century–Fox), *The Devil's Bedroom* (Manson Distributing Corp. [also director, coproducer], *Iron Angel* (Ken Kennedy Productions)
1965 *Major Dundee* (Columbia)
1968 *Hang 'em High* (United Artists), *Stay Away Joe* (MGM)
1969 *Backtrack* (Universal), *The Wild Bunch* (Warner Bros.–Seven Arts), *Witchmaker* (Excelsior Distributing) [executive producer]
1970 *The Ballad of Cable Hogue* (Warner Bros.), *The McMasters* (Chevron)
1971 *The Hunting Party* (United Artists), *Brotherhood of Satan* (Columbia) [also coproducer]
1973 *Pat Garrett & Billy the Kid* (MGM)
1974 *The Richard Petty Story* (Rowland–Lasko)
1975 *White Line Fever* (Columbia), *Winterhawk* (Howco International)
1976 *Mother, Jugs and Speed* (20th Century–Fox), *A Boy and His Dog* (Marvin Distributors) [director, screenwriter, coproducer]
1979 *Fast Charlie ... The Moonbeam Rider* (Universal)
1981 *The Beast Within*

Strother Martin

1950 *The Asphalt Jungle* (MGM)
1955 *The Big Knife* (United Artists)
1956 *Attack!* (United Artists)
1958 *Cowboy* (Columbia)
1959 *The Horse Soldiers* (United Artists)
1961 *Sanctuary* (20th Century–Fox), *The Deadly Companions* (Pathe–American)
1962 *The Man Who Shot Liberty Valance* (Paramount)
1963 *Showdown* (Universal), *McLintock* (United Artists)
1964 *Invitation to a Gunfighter* (United Artists)
1965 *The Sons of Katie Elder* (Paramount), *Brainstorm* (Warner Bros.), *Shenandoah* (Universal)
1966 *Harper* (Warner Bros.), *An Eye for an Eye* (Embassy)
1967 *Cool Hand Luke* (Warner Bros.–Seven Arts), *The Flim-Flam Man* (20th Century–Fox)
1969 *True Grit* (Paramount), *Butch Cassidy and the Sundance Kid* (20th Century–Fox), *The Wild Bunch* (Warner Bros.–Seven Arts)
1970 *The Ballad of Cable Hogue* (Warner Bros.)
1971 *Fool's Parade* (Columbia), *Brotherhood of Satan* (Columbia), *Red Sky at Morning* (Universal)
1972 *Hannie Caulder* (Paramount), *Pocket Money* (National General)
1973 *Sssssss* (Universal)
1975 *Hard Times* (Columbia), *Rooster Cogburn* (Universal)
1976 *Great Scout and Cathouse Thursday* (American-International)
1977 *Slap Shot* (Universal)
1978 *The End* (United Artists)
1979 *The Champ* (United Artists), *Nightwing* (Columbia), *The Villain* (Columbia), *Up in Smoke* (Paramount), *Love and Bullets* (ITC Entertainment Ltd.)

Bill McKinney

1967 *She Freak* (Sonney–Friedman Pictures)
1968 *The Road Hustlers* (American-International)
1970 *Angel Unchained* (American-International)
1972 *Deliverance* (Warner Bros.), *Junior Bonner* (Cinerama), *The Life and Times of Judge Roy Bean* (National General), *Kansas City Bomber* (MGM)
1973 *Cleopatra Jones* (Warner Bros.)
1974 *The Outfit* (United Artists), *Thunderbolt and Lightfoot* (United Artists), *The Parallax View* (Paramount), *For Pete's Sake* (Columbia)
1976 *Cannonball* (New World), *The Outlaw Josey Wales* (Warner Bros.), *The Shootist* (Paramount)
1977 *The Gauntlet* (Warner Bros.), *Valentino* (United Artists)
1978 *Every Which Way But Loose* (Warner Bros.)

(Bill McKinney, *cont.*)

1979 *When You Comin' Back, Red Ryder?* (Columbia)
1980 *Bronco Billy* (Warner Bros.), *Carny* (United Artists)
1981 *Any Which Way You Can* (Warner Bros.)
1982 *Tex* (Buena Vista)

Andrew Robinson

1972 *Dirty Harry* (Warner Bros.)
1973 *Charley Varrick* (Universal)
1975 *Mackintosh & T.J.* (Penland), *The Drowning Pool* (Warner Bros.)

Lee Van Cleef

1952 *High Noon* (United Artists), *Untamed Frontier* (Universal-International)
1953 *Beast from 20,000 Fathoms* (Warner Bros.), *Vice Squad* (United Artists), *The Nebraskan* (Columbia), *Arena* (MGM)
1954 *Gypsy Colt* (MGM), *Arrow in the Dust* (Allied Artists), *Yellow Tomahawk* (United Artists), *Rails into Laramie* (Universal-International), *Dawn at Soccoro* (Universal), *Princess of the Nile* (20th Century–Fox)
1955 *Ten Wanted Men* (Columbia), *The Big Combo* (Allied Artists), *Treasure of Ruby Hills* (Allied Artists), *I Cover the Underworld* (Republic), *Road to Denver* (Republic), *A Man Alone* (Republic)
1956 *The Conqueror* (RKO Radio), *Tribute to a Badman* (MGM), *Pardners* (Paramount)
1957 *Gunfight at the OK Corral* (Paramount), *Joe Dakota* (Universal), *China Gate* (20th Century–Fox), *Tin Star* (Paramount)
1958 *The Young Lions* (20th Century–Fox), *The Bravados* (20th Century–Fox)
1959 *Guns, Girls and Gangsters* (United Artists)
1961 *Posse from Hell* (Universal)
1962 *The Man Who Shot Liberty Valance* (Paramount)
1963 *How the West Was Won* (MGM-Cinerama)
1965 *For a Few Dollars More* (United Artists)
1967 *The Good, the Bad, and the Ugly* (United Artists)
1968 *The Big Gundown* (Columbia)
1969 *Death Rides a Horse* (United Artists), *Day of Anger* (National General)
1970 *Sabata* (United Artists), *Barquero* (United Artists), *El Condor* (National General)
1971 *Captain Apache* (Scotia International)
1972 *The Magnificent Seven Ride* (United Artists)
1973 *Return of Sabata* (United Artists)

1975 *Take a Hard Ride* (20th Century–Fox), *Power Kill* (Aquarius),
     Bad Man's River (Scotia International)
1976 *Mean Frank and Crazy Tony* (Aquarius), *The Stranger and the
     Gunfighter* (Columbia), *Crime Boss* (Cinema Shares Inter-
     national)
1977 *Kid Vengeance* (Irwin Yablans)
1979 *God's Gun* (Irwin Yablans)
1981 *The Octagon* (American Cinema), *Escape from New York* (Avco–
     Embassy)

Index

(Page numbers in **bold** indicate photos)

www.ingramcontent.com/pod-product-compliance
Ingram Content Group UK Ltd.
Pitfield, Milton Keynes, MK11 3LW, UK
UKHW041355190726
13851UKWH00014B/126